MW00469086

DOWN
to the
SEA AGAIN

Jim & Angie George

Down to the Sea Again

©2022 Jim George

All rights reserved. This book or any portion thereof may not be reproduced or used in any manner whatsoever without the express written permission of the publisher except for the use of brief quotations in a book review.

print ISBN: 978-1-66785-074-0

ebook ISBN: 978-1-66785-075-7

Contents

In memory of our friend Tad Weed,
who lived his dreams in his music.

Heraclitus:

You cannot step twice into the same rivers;
for other waters are ever flowing on to you.

"Do It Soon"

Every time Angie spotted a Hinckley sailboat, she would point it out, exclaiming how beautiful it was. This was back in the mid 1980s when we were living aboard our Tartan 30 *Escapade* and cruising the East Coast and the Bahamas. Ever since that time, when anyone politely asked, "Is there anything I can do for you?" she was apt to respond, "Buy me a Hinckley yacht." It was a double jest. Hinckleys, the Rolls Royces of American built sailboats, were far out of our reach financially. And after our year long seagoing adventure, we had gone back to work and developed new interests. We had taken up wilderness and white water canoeing and gone on long camping trips throughout much of Mexico, the U.S. and the maritime provinces of Canada. Occasionally we talked about going back to sea again, or maybe buying a converted lobster boat and cruising up and down the Intracoastal Waterway on the East Coast. This was just one of many dreams, like living in France or Italy for several months or a year, or taking a trip around the world.

So in September of 2012, when we were renting a cottage in Southwest Harbor on Mt. Desert Island, I mentioned to Angie that this was the home of Hinckley Yachts, and maybe we should look at one. There happened to be a 45 foot Hinckley yawl for sale in the Hinckley yard and so we asked the broker if we could look at her. She was as beautiful inside as she was out, with her sumptuous accommodations and mahogany woodwork. We told the broker we were seriously thinking of going cruising again, but that this boat was too big and too expensive for us. The owner would probably accept a lower price, he told us. "He's a rich doctor, but he's seventy-five years old and getting too old for sailing." "I'm older than that," I told him. The broker looked at me, and without a pause came back, "You'd better do it soon!" No, we didn't buy the Hinckley. The truth is that we were already negotiating to buy a cruising sailboat, and we were planning to "do it soon."

It had been almost 27 years since we returned from our year living aboard *Escapade*. Could this old man and his (much younger!) mate go back to the cruising life after all this time? The boat would be bigger, providing many more comforts but also more challenging to handle. With GPS and modern chart plotters and other electronics, navigation should be a cinch, but the learning curve would be pretty steep for an old codger who grew up when even television was a novelty. On the other hand, we were both (thank all the gods that be) in good health, physically fit, and still in command of (most of) our mental faculties. Going back to sea had been something we'd talked about for years—really ever since we returned from our first big sailing adventure—but there was always some reason we didn't do it. We didn't want to sell or rent out our house, we had acquired two cats that we couldn't bear parting with, we were having such a good time on canoe expeditions, or traveling around in our van, the list goes on and on. There was always "Some day. . ." But more and more and more of our friends were dying or becoming incapacitated by illness.

Then one day Angie said, "Let's do it!" and all of the obstacles began to melt away. So we began our search for a boat.

"Sea-Fever"

I must down to the seas again, to the lonely sea and the sky,
And all I ask is a tall ship and a star to steer her by,
And the wheel's kick and the wind's song and the white sail's shaking,
And a grey mist on the sea's face, and a grey dawn breaking.

I must down to the seas again, for the call of the running tide
Is a wild call and a clear call that may not be denied;
And all I ask is a windy day with the white clouds flying,
And the flung spray and the blown spume, and the sea-gulls crying.

I must down to the seas again, to the vagrant gypsy life,
To the gull's way and the whale's way where the wind's like a whetted knife;
And all I ask is a merry yarn from a laughing fellow-rover
And quiet sleep and a sweet dream when the long trick's over.

John Masefield (1878-1967).
(English Poet Laureate, 1930-1967.)

PART ONE:
ESCAPADE

Chapter One:

How It All Began

Jim: I had been dreaming and scheming to go to sea for most of my adult life. I read every book by Eric and Susan Hiscock, as well as by every other world sailor that I could get my hands on. I learned to sail dinghies on fickle winded ponds, and every chance I got, I volunteered to crew on cruising boats racing on the Great Lakes. Eventually my wife and I bought our own cruising boat, a Cal 25, which we named *Windhover* after the poem by Gerard Manley Hopkins. We began spending our summer breaks from teaching school cruising Lake Michigan and Lake Huron, especially the beautiful Georgian Bay and North Channel areas of Lake Huron. Our next boat was a Tartan 30, *Escapade*, which I dreamed was boat enough, if not to take us around the world, at least to let us experience the challenges of ocean sailing. Unfortunately, though we'd always managed to avoid the rocky hazards of the northern Great Lakes, our marriage didn't fare so well, and we ended up divorcing. She got the house and I got the boat.

My friend Mike and I had already talked of taking a year off from our jobs, and taking *Escapade* out to the Atlantic. Mike and I had both learned to sail at the University of Michigan Sailing Club, and though he was fifteen years younger than I, we got along well together. We had sailed together on the Great Lakes, and I knew that he was a competent sailor as well as a good companion. But somehow, after the divorce, I lost my motivation and the dream began to dry up. Meanwhile I was dating, trying to juggle my relationships with my two young adult children, and struggling to keep my head above water on my teaching job. I had never hung out in bars much, but one Friday afternoon I dropped into Mr. Flood's Party. That turned out to be a life changing decision.

Angie: Even as a small child I was interested in boats. My mother would take us down to the locks in Sault Ste. Marie, Michigan, to watch the lake freighters go through. I was fascinated by the crews skillfully handling the gigantic lines (I later learned they are called hawsers) holding the ships as they were raised or lowered in the locks. Little did I know that some thirty years later this, on a smaller scale, would be my job as we transited the Welland and the Erie canals in a thirty foot sailboat. It wouldn't have happened if I hadn't been in the practice of hanging out on Friday afternoons with my teacher and townie friends at a local Ann Arbor bar appropriately named Mr. Flood's Party.

Mr. Flood's Party

Jim: I stood there in the crowded bar looking around to see who was there that I knew. It was Friday afternoon, and this was not just any bar. Mr. Flood's Party attracted a whole cross section of Ann Arborites, from doctors and lawyers to unregenerated hippies, and everything in between. We came to drink beer, listen to country and western music, eat peanuts, throwing the shells on the floor, and most importantly, rub elbows with old and new friends.

I had never been one for going to bars much, except to listen to jazz, but I was recently divorced and looking for warmth and fellowship on a cold February afternoon. So I stood in the doorway, listening to the Cadillac Cowboys on the stage to my left, and taking in the people sitting at the long polished wooden bar with a moose head hanging over it. Right in front of me was a tall lanky guy with a face rough hewn like Abraham Lincoln's. I would have recognized him anywhere. It was Jay Stielstra, a local singer, songwriter, and playwright who also happened to be a fellow teacher. The petite woman Jay was talking to had her back to me, but I was struck by her long, almost black, curly hair.

I can't say that I was adept at talking to strange women. I was married at nineteen to the girl I had dated as a senior in high school, and I'd only had a couple of girlfriends before that. Since my divorce, I'd dated a couple of women, but both were people I'd known for many years. But I was ready to take the plunge, try to overcome my natural shyness and talk to someone new. So when Jay left his seat (I knew Jay was happily married and not romantically interested in this woman), I sat down. The woman, of course, was Angie.

Angie: When I caught sight out of the corner of my eye of this tall, slender, good looking guy with a salt and pepper Afro and beard, I took notice. When Jay left Jim took Jay's empty seat and we started talking, noting that I, too, was a teacher in the same school system.

Jim: I don't remember what we talked about, but she was easy to talk to. The fact that we were both teachers probably provided fodder for some of our conversation. And we had some mutual friends, but I don't think we discovered how many or how much our interests overlapped until later. I do remember how the encounter ended. A woman I had been dating came up and reminded me that we had a dinner date that evening.

Angie: We'd been chatting for a while when a tall blonde woman came along and reminded Jim that they had a dinner date that evening. Of course, I immediately thought that Jim was taken. After she left, Jim explained that he was breaking up with her. Yeah, I believed that. I told him that I was no home wrecker and that I had to leave and meet up with some friends.

Jim: I cringed when Angie said that. I had been trying to break up with B____ for some time, but she wasn't letting go. On paper she would have been the perfect match for me. She was an avid sailor (and sailing had been my passion for 20 years), an excellent cook, liked books and music . . . but somehow I was very uncomfortable with her. We'd had this dinner date planned for a while, and although she already knew how I felt, I thought this time I could convince her that it was really over between us. I was sorry to see Angie go, but she did ask me if I wanted her phone number before she left.

"Are you in the book?" I asked (this shows what a smoothie I was).

"Yes," she answered, looking a little puzzled.

"Well, I can look you up."

Angie: When Jim didn't take my phone number (that was new for me), I thought I probably would never hear from him again. I don't know why Jim stayed on my mind. Jim was older than me and I was used to dating men who were younger and on the wild side. But there was something about Jim's quietness that attracted me. During the conversation at Mr. Flood's Party we had talked about Sunday jazz at the Del Rio bar. I was friends with one of the owners, Ernie Harburg, and Jim was friends with Rick Burgess, the other owner. So I thought that if I went to the Del Rio the next Sunday I might run into Jim again.

Jim: I was sitting at the bar in the Del Rio listening to the band when I noticed Angie and a friend of hers standing near the doorway. The place was crowded and I figured they were probably looking for a place to sit down. Angie left her friend and came down to the bar where I was sitting.

"Do you remember me?" she asked. I can see why she thought I might not, since she'd had a rather drastic haircut since I'd seen her last.

"Sure," I said. "In fact, I tried to call you this morning."

"Yeah, I believe that!" she laughed. You have to remember that this was before voice mail, and answering machines were not even that common.

"Is this your number?" I asked, and I rattled off her number.

So that's the story of how our relationship started. When people ask how we met, I always say, "She picked me up in a bar." Angie doesn't think that's quite an accurate way to describe it.

Chapter Two:

The North Channel

Angie: When I met Jim in 1982. one of my first questions for him was, "Do you like Shakespeare?" "I *teach* Shakespeare," he said. Then he came back with, "Do you get seasick?" I didn't have much experience being on boats, so I replied "No." Jim's dream was to someday take an extended cruise, perhaps around the world.

Shortly after we met, Jim invited me for a day sail on Lake Erie, where he kept *Escapade*. I didn't get seasick, but as I jumped onto the dock to secure the boat as we came into her slip at the marina I slipped and sprained my ankle. I crawled to the cleat and managed to secure the line to the cleat. I was embarrassed and wondered if Jim would ever ask me to go sailing again.

Well he did, in fact he invited me to join him and some friends for a week sailing the North Channel of Lake Huron. In the summer the North Channel and Georgian Bay areas of Lake Huron are a mini paradise. The water is crystal clear and you can look down and see rocks thirty feet below the surface. Anchoring in secluded harbors surrounded by the rocks and forests of the Canadian countryside, picking wild blueberries, swimming in the cold water, buying and cooking fresh perch—these are some of my memories of that first cruise in the

North Channel. Jim dropped me off in the Soo and picked up the crew, including the same blonde that he was supposedly breaking up with, for the next leg of his cruise. I hadn't thought about how I would get back to Ann Arbor and had to have my dad wire me money. When I tell the story I always say that Jim dumped me off in the Soo.

Jim: As most people would, I experienced some mood swings after my divorce, but it was always refreshing to be around Angie. Her bright outlook and cheerful disposition never failed to cheer me up, and soon we were dating regularly. My friend Mike and I had been planning to take a year off from work and take an extended cruise. Angie and I had probably been dating for a little over a year when I told her that I had changed my mind about that trip. She looked at me and said, "You have to go. You've been preparing for this for the last 20 years!" I looked at her and responded, "Will you go with me?" It took her a nano-second to answer "Yes!"

After Angie accepted my offer to take a year off from our jobs and go sailing, we decided that it would be wise for us to spend a summer together on the boat to find out just how compatible we were. So in July of 1984 we left the marina in Lake Erie and headed for the North Channel of Lake Huron.

The North Channel, formed by islands off the Canadian shore of Lake Huron, is one of the most beautiful sailing areas in the world. Protected anchorages among primeval forests and pre-Cambrian rocks inhabited by abundant wildlife attract thousands of sailors and boaters. Even so it was still possible to find isolated coves to tuck yourself into where you can experience the joy of private communion with the natural world.

After my son and daughter helped us pilot the boat up through the Detroit and St. Clair rivers and then the length of Lake Huron to

Tobermory on the tip of the Bruce Peninsula in Canada, Angie and I set off alone to explore the harbors and coves of the North Channel.

Our first stop, after sailing through water so clear that you could see the rocks thirty feet down, was Cove Island, only five miles from Tobermory. The Cove was as beautiful as I remembered it from my solo visit two years earlier, herons dotting the shore and the sound of fish jumping and ospreys in the tree tops. But the next morning we were joined by several other boats, including a power boat with some fairly obnoxious nude sunbathers on deck, so we went looking for a spot where we could have some privacy. I had long wanted to explore the second cove on Cove Island, seldom visited by any but fishermen in small boats. The chart makes the entrance look very unpromising and it is not mentioned in the cruising guides. We took the dinghy with the new 2 h.p. motor that Angie had bought for us to check it out, and after getting information on depths and obstacles from a local fisherman, found that with care we could bring *Escapade* in. We anchored in 8 to 10 feet of water with a beaver dam at our back door. I got up early in the morning hoping to see the inhabitant, but he was not making an appearance. Then when I went forward to pay my morning respects to Neptune, I heard a tremendous Whack! on the water. Looking over toward the hut, I could see where he had given his danger signal and dove. I didn't see him again.

From Jim's journal: "This place is marvelous! Yesterday Angie and I went exploring. We tried both north and south of the cove to find trails. We found a clear spot to go ashore and forged a couple of hundred yards through the bush, but then it got so wild that we thought we might get lost, so we came back. We had better luck at the east end, where the bay narrows down to a kind of creek. We followed the creek as far as we could in the dinghy, then climbed out and headed east on foot. The creek was really a cut that ended up in a great moraine with a tiny trickle of water down the middle. With a little more water you could have taken a dinghy right out to the bay. On the bay side we found a great pile of logs that could have been mistaken for the work of a beaver except that there were nails in them. Somebody had built something there, but then abandoned it to the elements. There was also what looked like a slab from the side of a ship—several ribs with planking on them looking like they had been hand-hewn. You could imagine the lone survivor of a shipwreck having landed here. The spot is called Tecumseh Cove."

After some more exploring on foot we took the dinghy and carefully charted the entrance to what we thought of as our secret cove. As we were exploring we saw a giant bird flying across the bay. When it landed in a treetop we could see the horns that identified it as a great horned owl. While we watched it, two terns dove at it, driving it into the woods.

The next night was a howler! A cold front swept through with thunderstorms in the early evening. I was glad to see that the plow anchor* was dug in good and would hold us because the wind shifted to the northwest and we were only about two or three boat lengths off the lee shore. I slept all night with one ear open. I kept thinking that I should have set another anchor earlier. Being driven on to the shore is one of the worst thing that can happen to a sailboat, but I had checked the plow and it was really dug in. Good anchoring is one of the most important skills that a cruising sailor needs for the safety of the crew and the boat. We learned a lot more about this when we took *Escapade* out to the East Coast.

While we were in our private little cove, we decided to inventory the boat so that we would know what we needed to add for our upcoming yearlong trip. The list we made was four and a half pages long, double columned, and that didn't include food. When you include every light, battery, piece of navigation equipment, radio, etc., there's a lot of stuff on a boat. Angie commented that I sure have a lot of toys. I guess that was true when you think of the guitar, ham radio, camera—not to mention *Escapade* herself.

When the inventory was finished we went ashore to see if we could make it across to the other bay, Cove Island Harbour proper. Our path was a beaver trail, and it was good trail—if you were one foot tall. We managed to cut our way through to the harbor, a short hike as that's where the beaver wanted to go, too. We stood and gazed at the bay for a while and felt like discoverers, since there was no one anchored there.

The next day we had a joyful spinnaker* run to Covered Portage Cove, a beautiful anchorage surrounded by tall white rocky cliffs. As we approached the mainland and out of the influence of Lake Huron, it got warmer and we stripped down to shorts and T-shirts. After we had anchored and tied to my favorite tree off my favorite rock, we took showers on the foredeck together (in our bathing suits—there were other boats in the harbor).

---

* An asterisk marks words or terms explained in the glossary.

Escapade in Covered Portage Cove

Covered Portage is one of the most picturesque spots in the North Channel, but what a change from Cove Island. First of all there were eighteen boats anchored there. And the North Channel mosquitoes were out in full force. Shortly after the sun sets, around 9:15 in the evening, the first one came buzzing around. Up went the screens. Fifteen minutes later the screens were covered with mosquitoes lusting for our blood. Their buzzing sounded like an airplane flying over. The North Channel mosquitoes arrive predictably a few minutes after sundown, and they come in droves. If you don't get the screens up in time, it's misery all night long.

Not only did Angie prove to be a great sailing companion, but she is a fine cook. She soon upended my tradition of instant coffee, canned corn beef hash, and red beans and rice. (We kept the red beans and rice in our repertoire, but the rest, including a canned whole chicken, was history.) Our meals now included pasta with her incomparable spaghetti sauce, a recipe learned from her Italian mother and grandmother, chicken parmesan, and best of all, blueberry pie made with the wild blueberries we gathered while exploring the rocky shores around our anchorages. We learned how to bake on top of the alcohol stove, and Angie took full advantage of it.

I had canceled my plans to go off sailing for a year with my friend Mike, but Angie's enthusiasm rekindled my interest. She was an eager learner and spent much of her time, while we sailed from harbor to harbor with Elmer (our automatic helm) steering the boat, practicing knots. She was soon adept with the bowline, clove hitch, and rolling hitch, all indispensable when working with a boat's lines. More important, she proved to be a great sailing partner. She was eager to learn everything about the boat. She spurred me on to keep things clean and in order, and that makes life more pleasant. She liked sailing and soon learned to handle the boat in all kinds of conditions. She especially liked beating* in a good wind, with the boat "on its ear," as she liked to say. Most important, she is good natured, and didn't get upset when things went wrong, and that helped keep me in a good mood. I began to develop a really positive feeling that the "big journey" south would really happen. At 48 I felt like a kid again.

After our summer together on *Escapade* in the North Channel and on Lake Huron, Angie and I decided that if we could get along together for two months living on thirty foot boat it was time to move in together. So we did and began the serious work of getting the boat ready to go to sea. It seemed that almost daily the UPS man arrived with something new for the boat. Charts and books on navigation, spare parts, a bladder to increase our water capacity—these were just some of the things we needed to make a successful trip. We had made list after list of items we needed and jobs that needed doing—and checked it more than twice. By the end of June we had packed all of our worldly goods not related to sailing, put them in storage and vacated our apartment. Passing by the apartment for the last time, we picked up our final UPS package of backordered supplies. This was some 5/8 inch hose which we needed to complete the installation of the spare fifteen gallon water tank. There were a few more jobs to do, but if sailors waited until every little thing was in order before setting sail, they would never leave port.

Chapter Three:

The Great Lakes

Our projected route to the sea involved crossing Lake Erie from one end to the other, negotiating the locks on the Welland Canal connecting the two lakes, then sailing Lake Ontario end to end. On the east end of Lake Ontario, we would enter the Erie canal system, which would take us to the Hudson River near Albany. Then down the Hudson to New York City, where we would meet the ocean.

Angie: I count Sunday, June 30 1985, as the beginning of the most exciting and joyful year of my life, even though we didn't get off to a great start. We left our slip at the Toledo Beach Marina on Lake Erie at 11:00 with Jim's daughter Kari aboard as an extra crew member. Lake Erie is shallow, especially at the west end, and even a light wind could produce a nasty chop. As we headed out into the east wind and we went to raise the mainsail, the halyard slipped from Jim's hand and began swinging wildly in the air. Jim thought he was going to have to climb the mast to retrieve it, but Kari managed to catch it as it swung past her. Soon the main was up, with a double reef* in it, and we were clipping along at five knots, not quite in the direction of our target. Escapade sailed beautifully, but the chop was short and steep, often sending green water over our deck. In a half hour we were all feeling a bit squeamish.

When we reached West Sister Island, we discussed anchoring in the lee of the island and going on to Put-In-Bay on South Bass Island the next day. But the wind faired, allowing us to almost lay Put-In-Bay, and we were sailing along at a good five knots, so we carried on despite our queasy stomachs. Three hours later, in the smoother waters in the lee of Bass Island and a short tack* from Put-In-Bay, we were glad we'd made that choice. We'd sailed forty miles in a little over seven hours. We felt set free of our home port—water gypsies at last.

But we weren't to be spared embarrassment. As we proudly entered the harbor under sail, I felt *Escapade* come to a stop. Jim had misjudged the harbor entrance and we were aground. We lowered the sails, and Jim got an anchor ready to kedge* off. A fisherman came by in a power boat, and I thought he would offer to help us, but instead he sped by hollering, "Get a chart!"

Jim: [Journal entry: July 3, 1985 1200 hours] I am sitting in the cockpit with my leg propped up against the companionway hatch, a bag of ice wrapped to my shin. *Escapade* is moving along at four and a half knots in a nice westerly breeze. We'd be doing six with the spinnaker up, but I'm favoring my leg until the swelling goes down. There's a lump the size of a goose egg under the ice pack.

Angie was a bit nervous about making a straight shot from Bass Island to Port Collins, at the east end of Lake Erie, 180 miles and at least 36 hours of sailing, but the weather report was for the high to continue, and we decided to go for it. It would be our first overnight passage, and having Kari aboard would make it easier. We split watches, with Angie and Kari taking 7 to 10 and 2 to 5. The night watches were uneventful. We sailed along quietly on a broad reach,* and we even had a full moon for part of the night.

When I came topside to take over at five, the wind had died and Angie and Kari had furled the big Jenny* and started the engine. Shortly after I took over the helm, just about sunrise, the breeze came up again. I unfurled the Jenny and to my dismay found that it was covered with ugly green spots. There had been a hatch of mayflies during the night, and when the wind died the crew couldn't see that the bugs were covering the sail. The bugs were mashed all over the sail when it was furled. The boat was sailing along smoothly on a broad reach under the guidance of Elmer, our autohelm,* so I decided to try to rinse the sail. I tied a line to a bucket and began dipping it in the water and throwing the water up on the sail. As I threw the third bucket of water, the boat rocked gently and I stepped off the edge of the boat. The netting attached to the lifelines kept me from going overboard, but my leg was trapped between the netting and the boat. My shin hit the gunnel at the edge of the deck, and hence the goose egg. After my unsuccessful dingbat attempt to wash the bugs off the sail by throwing water at them (and after my wound had been dressed), Angie and I took the sail down and tried washing it with Woolite and Spray and Wash, dragging it in the water to rinse it. It looked better, but not all of the stains came out.

Lake Erie has been an infestation of bugs. Coming out of Put-In-Bay we had a nice spinnaker run if it hadn't been for the plague of flies. They look like houseflies, but they bite and will drive you insane—"the very devil's curse," as songwriter Jay Stielstra called them. Today so far we have fewer of the biting ones, but thousands of little ones that stick to you and then die when you brush them away. They are cannibalistic, and five or six go for the dead one's corpse. They make a godawful mess. We've cleaned the boat twice since yesterday, and it's filthy again.

[Jim's Journal, July 4, 1985] Lake Erie is pretty here at the east end. We are sailing in 145 feet of water, the sun is out, there are small white caps, and the water has turned from greenish brown to the deep blue of northern Lakes Huron and Michigan. The lake is nearly deserted—we have seen only two freighters since yesterday morning. We are unable to see shore except for a few lights last night. We could be on the ocean, except for what the depth sounder is telling us.

[July 5, 1985 1900 hours] The last leg across Lake Erie was a galloping run. We flew the spinnaker until I got nervous and decided it was time to take it down before we blew it out. The LORAN* was registering a boat speed of 7.5—the highest it's ever gone. As Angie took the boat into Port Colbourne, we were still doing over six. [That doesn't sound like much, but in a small sailboat it's exhilarating to say the least.] The waves looked as menacing as any we had seen on Lake Huron. Tomorrow we will face a new challenge as we make our way through the Welland Canal.

The Welland Canal
July 7, 1985

Jim: After crossing Lake Erie from end to end, we spent a day in Port Colbourne doing odd jobs and getting the boat and ourselves ready for transiting the eight locks of the Welland Canal. The canal, which the lake and ocean freighters use to go between Lake Ontario and Lake Erie, was our biggest challenge so far. Even though pleasure boats are grouped to go through together to avoid interference with commercial traffic, the 26 mile trip often takes twelve hours and can take as many as 24. In Port Colbourne we met two couples in Pearson 36's, *Wind*

Trails and *Bittersweet*, who were heading for the St. Lawrence. That put the bug in our ear that we might take that route to the ocean. It was farther than going by the Erie Canal, but it would save us taking our mast down and negotiating the 38 locks of the canal.

We arrived at the boat dock at the first lock at about 8 a.m. and were told that we would have about an hour to wait. While we waited a boat that had just come through gave us a bunch of straw bales to add to the two that we had bought in Port Colbourne. These were to protect the boat from scraping against the walls of the lock. We had enough to line both sides of *Escapade*. As it turned out, despite our worries, the transit went smoothly, and we moved through all eight locks and 26 miles of canal in six and a half hours. We felt pretty lucky.

Lake Ontario

From the Welland Canal we motored the three miles to Port Delhousey, where we bought a chart for Toronto. The chandler and a friend talked to us about the glories of the St. Lawrence, and we were again tempted to go that way. We decided to look for charts in Toronto and then make our decision.

Toronto was in a festive mood when we got there. The Molson Jazz festival was in full swing on the waterfront, the Italian Navy was visiting the port, and the harbor was filled with every imaginable type of sailing craft, including a Viking ship propelled by four stalwart oarsman. We got a kick out of watching four of the Italian sailors, short men in spanking white uniforms, study the pavilion featuring a wide variety of international foods and then zero in on the stand selling hamburgers and french fries. In Toronto we found Rebouf's Maps, which we had heard was the best chart store in Toronto. They had an amazing supply of maps and charts, but for the St. Lawrence they only had out to salt water—a little past Montreal. Getting charts for the maritime provinces on short notice seemed iffy, and rechecking the distance, we found it to be still more than 1200 miles from Montreal to Halifax. Disappointed, we scrapped the idea of going the seaway route, or rather we put it on the back burner. We hoped to do it on a later trip when we would be better prepared for it. When we did reach the ocean, and started learning to deal with tides, we were glad that our first experiences with them hadn't been on the St. Lawrence River.

Water

Angie: *Escapade* had a thirty gallon water tank. We knew that thirty gallons wasn't going to be enough to get by on living aboard, so Jim had ordered a 15 gallon rubber bladder to add to our supply. He hadn't had a chance to install it before we left home, so that became our project while we were in Toronto. I promised to help if Jim promised not to swear. Of course, asking a sailor not to swear is a hopeless cause, and I became an expert at it myself. Whenever you do a job on a sailboat, you end up turning yourself into a contortionist because you never have enough space to maneuver. The bladder was going to go in one of the cockpit lockers,* and somehow we needed to feed a hose from the cockpit locker, underneath the starboard quarter berth,* through the galley, and up to the sink. When Jim drilled a hole through the bulkhead between the cockpit locker and the quarter berth, he got it too high and drilled into the quarter berth cushion. Fortunately, this was just a test hole, and he got it drilled properly. Then he had to put a hole down from the locker under the sink. He was nervous about this one, because if he miscalculated, he'd be drilling through the bottom of the boat. It turned out OK and we didn't sink and I didn't jump ship.

It was easy to feed the hose from the bladder through the quarter berth locker to the galley. The hard part was to get it under the galley and up to the sink hose connection. We straightened out a hanger and

Jim poked it through from the quarter berth while I fished for it with a loop in a piece of whipping line. I caught it and then Jim pulled the line through. We tied the line to the hose with a rolling hitch (one of the "must know" knots that Jim taught me) and pulled it through to the sink. It worked! Jim, Kari, and I formed a bucket brigade to fill the bladder with fresh water. We added a gallon of vinegar and let it set for a week, and then, Voila!, we'd increased our water supply to an amazing 45 gallons. Jim was proud of himself, because this was the biggest renovation that he'd undertaken on the boat.

Well, you can imagine that 45 gallons of water isn't a lot to get by on when you figure it has to cover all of your cooking, cleaning up, bathing, etc. (In the Bahamas we added two five gallon jerry cans to bring our capacity to 55 gallons. We later carried 150 gallons on *Bel Canto*.) For showers we used shore facilities whenever we could, but that wasn't alway possible. And in some places on the East Coast they charged up to ten dollars for showers, enough to break our twenty-five dollar a day budget! So we used a two and half gallon sun shower to take showers aboard the boat. That was a gallon and a quarter for each of us, and if you don't think that's a challenge, try it some time. You get wet, soap up the vital areas, then rinse. We called this a "sailor's shower," and it worked really well. Jim would hang the shower from a spare halyard and we would bathe in the cockpit, in the nude if there was no one around, or wearing our swim suits if there was a crowd. When we were coming down the Hudson we were anchored in the mooring area of the yacht club at the Tappan Zee bridge. I had stripped and was taking a shower when out of the corner of my eye I caught a glimpse of a sailboat with four guys ghosting quietly across our stern. I noticed the sly grins on their faces as I grabbed a shirt to put on. They turned and came back to tell us that we were anchored in the club's fairway* and would probably experience a lot of traffic if we stayed there. They invited us to take a guest mooring and me to take a shower in their clubhouse. I thanked them but finished taking my shower with my bathing suit on. I can imagine them relating the story to their friends in the clubhouse about the woman they had encountered taking a shower in the nude.

In the Bahamas we had to buy water, which cost from ten to 25 cents a gallon, so any chance we got to get fresh water free, we took advantage of it. Sometimes we would find a cistern where we could dip water for our tanks, but that didn't happen often. When it rained we would try to collect the water that came down the mast. Jim would make a trough by reversing the mainsail cover and put a bucket at the end of the boom to catch the water. Sometimes in the middle of the night if we got a cloudburst I'd send Jim out to catch the water. Of course, if there was lightning we'd have to pass on that. We also learned that you could bathe in salt water using Lemon Joy for soap. When I was back teaching school in Ann Arbor, I would tell my students that I hadn't taken a shower for five months while in the Bahamas. They'd be grossed and incredulous until I told them about bathing with Lemon Joy.

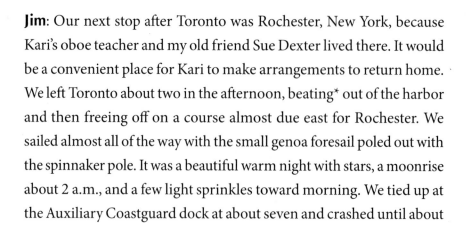

Jim: Our next stop after Toronto was Rochester, New York, because Kari's oboe teacher and my old friend Sue Dexter lived there. It would be a convenient place for Kari to make arrangements to return home. We left Toronto about two in the afternoon, beating* out of the harbor and then freeing off on a course almost due east for Rochester. We sailed almost all of the way with the small genoa foresail poled out with the spinnaker pole. It was a beautiful warm night with stars, a moonrise about 2 a.m., and a few light sprinkles toward morning. We tied up at the Auxiliary Coastguard dock at about seven and crashed until about

9:30. Angie was getting used to the long sails, and the possibility of going 55 miles seemed like a simple daysail. We then gave Sue a call and she brought her three children down to the marina—Leah, 7, Jon, 4 1/2, and Sara, four months. Leah had the same soulful look that I remembered her with as a baby. It was raining, but Jon was hot for a boat ride, so we cruised out to the end of the breakwater, then up to the drawbridge and back. Later Sue took us to her home, a beautiful old three story house near Park Avenue, a trendy section of Rochester.

Angie: Sue and her husband Bill Dexter treated us to a delicious chicken dinner. After dinner, while I was holding baby Sara, she decided to poop all over me. I had to strip and Sue washed all of my clothes, but that didn't stop me from holding Sara. They are a delightful family. We then said goodbye to Kari. It was moving because Jim wouldn't be seeing her for a long time, maybe a year. It was great having Kari along on the first part of the trip. She had grown from a passenger to a valuable crew member.

Chapter Four:

The Erie Canal

Escapade's route to the sea

Jim: We joined the Erie Canal at Oswego, New York, heading for Albany on the Hudson River. We found the public wall lined with boats that were either about to transit or had just finished transiting. The little marina there did a thriving business taking down and restepping* masts. (Because of the low bridge clearance along the Erie Canal, sailboats must remove their masts and carry them horizontally on the deck of the boat.) Some boat owners complained about the cost of

JIM & ANGIE GEORGE

$40, but I considered it cheap compared to what I was used to paying in the Detroit area. We had carried two-by-fours cut to size on deck all the way from Michigan to build stanchions to carry the mast. As I was working putting these together, an onlooker commented that I had to be a carpenter before starting my holiday. After installing the spare water bladder and rigging up a new VHF antenna on the stern rail, I thought, Yes, and an electrician and plumber, too. Anyway, George, the guy in charge of handling the boom for lifting the mast from the boat, was careful and fast, and we soon had it secured in the stanchions.

Some of the boaters that had just gone through the canals had horror stories about their trips. Now this reminds us of all of the people who had bear scare stories when we were camping or similar disaster stories about when we were whitewater canoeing. But we took the stories seriously and learned what we could from them. One of the story tellers was Peter, who, with his girlfriend, had just brought his big Morgan Out Islander up from Florida. He said that they had had difficulty fending off, and that the locks can bash a boat to pieces. Especially bad, he said, were gaping holes in the walls that could catch a boat's rail as she comes up. He had lost his masthead light when his mast, stored in stanchions on deck as ours would be, had hit the wall as the bow swung inward. Hearing this, I made sure to put the butt end of the mast forward when I stored ours.

*Escapade with mast in stanchions and festooned with straw bags
for transiting the Erie Canal*

Our first day locking through from Oswego to Lake Oneida wasn't bad. Another sailor, who'd described the passage as easy, told us his technique of tying a long line from the bow to the stern. We could then wrap a bight* of the line around rungs of the ladder on the wall of the lock and Angie could move it up or down while I managed the tiller as the boat was rising or lowering. That worked well, but the second lock didn't have a ladder, so we tried the same thing using a pole. This lock was more turbulent, and the bow of the boat swung toward the wall, the butt of the mast gently scraping the wall as it did. No damage was done, but the masthead light would have been gone if it had been on that end. After that we learned that by taking the bight further aft, near the end of the cabin, we could control the boat quite easily. Putting the boat in forward at idle speed also helped. Our routine was to slide gently up to the wall on the starboard side. Angie would stand with the rope in her hand, putting a bight around the ladder as I stopped the boat by gunning it in reverse. I would slip the boat back into forward and then take the rope while Angie hurried forward to make sure the bow didn't swing into the wall. This all happened very quickly and smoothly. Angie got high compliments for her crewing from the skippers of other boats locking through with us, most of whom had several crew members assisting them. I think they were a bit envious.

Once we got past Three River Point, where the Oswego, the Seneca, and the Oneida rivers meet, the biggest threat we had was from the power boats racing up and down the river. At Lock 23 we met a westbound skipper from Australia who said the powerboats made it worse than sailing on the ocean. The traffic reminded me of what it was like to take a sailboat up the Detroit and St. Clair rivers on a weekend. I had vowed never to do that again. The closer we got to Lake Oneida the worse it got. At one point the wake tossed by a passing powerboat was so bad that it caused the front stanchion holding the mast to collapse. I dreaded the thought of crossing Lake Oneida the next day, which was a Sunday, but as it turned out, that wasn't what I had to worry about.

Angie: Jim had told me that we had to pass through locks on the way to the sea, but I had no idea what that meant. Of course I had seen ships going through the Soo Locks in Sault Ste. Marie where I grew up, but I didn't know how you managed that in a small boat. Jim had been through the smaller lock on the Canadian side, going from Lake Huron to Lake Superior, but I hadn't been with him on those trips. I began to get my education when we reached the Welland Canal that connects Lake Erie to Lake Ontario. The water drops over three hundred feet going from Erie to Ontario. The Eight locks there are huge, built to accommodate ocean going vessels. Seven of them drop 46 feet each.

We were worried that we might have to share the locks with one of those ocean ships, but as it turned out the lock masters had the small sail and power boats go through together. It was a hectic and fascinating experience. The dock hands threw you lines and you had to fasten them around cleats while fending off from the rough and slimy walls to prevent damage to the boat.

After negotiating the eight locks on the Welland Canal, we still had 38 locks on the Erie Canal to go through. The locks on the Erie Canal are a lot smaller, and you don't have to contend with large ships. But you do have to contend with bridges that are too low to pass under with your mast up. The mast had to come down for the duration of our trip through the canal. This meant taking off the sails and storing them, coiling sheets* and halyards*, and loosening and securing the rigging. So when we went through the locks, we had to be sure that the mast didn't crash into the side of the lock and get damaged.

Now there were only two of us to do the job, with no dockhands to help, so it took some coordination. Jim would steer the boat into the lock and handle the stern line, while I handled the bow line. I mastered it and received compliments from other boaters. The stanchions holding the mast worked out well, except one time, on Lake Oneida, when we were constantly buzzed by speeding power boats. I was taking advantage of a rare opportunity to sunbathe on the foredeck when a power boat came too close, creating a big wake. The front stanchion collapsed and the mast crashed into the deck, almost on top of me. I swore like a sailor and shook my fist at the red-faced captain speeding away from us. That ended my idyllic afternoon. Together we got the stanchion back up and the mast in place, and it stayed that way for the rest of our trip through the canals.

Brewerton, New York
(Tuesday, July 16, 1985)

Angie: You've probably never heard of Brewerton, and believe me, you haven't missed a thing. We spent our first night here, planning to cross Lake Oneida the next day, and what was meant to be an overnight stay turned into a nightmare. After I helped Jim fix the mast cradle that had collapsed on our first day on the canal system, we walked into town to buy some beer and hamburger for dinner. Jim set up the little portable charcoal grill on the pier next to where *Escapade* was tied up, and I went below to make a salad. Suddenly I heard this thump and a blood curdling yell. I popped up into the companionway to see the cockpit spattered with blood. As Jim had stepped from the wall into the cockpit, his toe had caught on the lifeline, tripping him. He fell across the cockpit and hit his shin on the far side of the cockpit in the exact place that he had hurt it on Lake Erie. The pain was making him dizzy, and I put wet cloths on his forehead. I was very upset because I knew that we were in a place without medical facilities. We kept ice on the wound for five hours and Jim kept his leg propped up all night. I worried that they might have to amputate Jim's leg and that I would have to singleshand the boat for the rest of the trip.

The next morning, which happened to be Sunday, Jim could hardly put any weight on his leg. We thought he should get an x-ray. Jim tried to contact the keeper of the last lock we had passed through by VHF radio to see where he could get some medical help, but that didn't work. (Remember, this was before cell phones.) And the ham radio was useless for short distances. So much for thousands of dollars worth of fancy equipment, I told Jim. So I decided to walk into town to see what I could find out. I was hoping that the pharmacy would be open on Sunday.

I was a little nervous about walking into town by myself because when Jim and I had gone in for the hamburger and beer several young guys in pickups had honked at me. I emptied some valuables out of my purse in case I ran into difficulty and told Jim that if I wasn't back in a few hours to come rescue me, injured leg or not. I got to the pharmacy OK and luckily it was open. The pharmacist told me that there was a hospital in Syracuse 20 miles away. We could take an ambulance there but we would have to get our own way back. Or there was a healthcare center four miles away, but it would be closed on Sunday. The pharmacist suggested that the next morning I should hang around Angelo's, the coffee shop across the street, and try to find a ride. I asked the clerk at the pharmacy if she knew anyone who could take us to the healthcare center. She said if she had a car she would, but that her son had her car. She didn't know of anyone else who could take us.

As I was walking back to the boat, feeling down, I felt a car slowing down beside me. I became nervous thinking of the guys who had been honking at me. But when I saw that it was a woman about my age with a child in the car I relaxed. She said that she had overheard my conversation with the pharmacist and that she wanted to volunteer her services. She told me that she had been in a similar situation and knew how I felt. I was relieved and told her I would meet her at the pharmacy the next day at 9 o'clock. She gave me her name, Barb, and her address and telephone number. We managed to get through the day. Jim got some writing done, we played some cribbage, and I cooked us a barbecued chicken dinner (and nearly got carried away by the mosquitoes while I was doing it). The kids here were even more annoying than the mosquitoes. They swam where our boat was moored and their favorite sport was throwing rocks in the water around us. They yelled a lot and had a limited vocabulary, mostly consisting of the word "Fuckass." By nighttime Jim was in great pain. He took some codeine and was able to get some sleep.

First thing in the morning Barb was at the end of the pier with a pair of crutches for Jim. He was feeling a little better, able to put some weight on his leg. He hobbled to the car using one crutch to help him walk. The women in the office at the health center in Central Square brought out my Calabrese. When we told them why we were there, they said "We're not taking new patients." We tried to explain that we were on a boat and that this was an emergency. "You said that it happened Saturday," they replied, "so it's not an emergency. You can go to the hospital at Syracuse." "We don't have a way to get to Syracuse," I said, fuming. "Well, how did you get here?" Jim and Barb got me out of there before I did something drastic. As we were leaving, Barb said she would take us to Syracuse. Then one of the women mentioned that there was a walk-in clinic 10 minutes away. Why didn't you tell us that right away, I thought.

At the walk-in clinic everyone was very friendly. They x-rayed his leg and found that nothing was broken. He did have an infection, though, and they prescribed a powerful antibiotic. That visit cost $90, which Jim put on Visa hoping that his health insurance from school would cover it. Barb took us to a drugstore in the mall, and we found that the prescription would cost another $30. Altogether that equalled about five days of our budget. It's a good thing that we have an emergency fund!

While Jim was waiting in back for the prescription, I was up front buying some Tampons. He motioned me to come back where he was standing and pointed to the Kotex. We could use this to make a shin guard for his injured leg. I picked out a box of mini-pads and brought them up to the clerk. Since I had already paid for the Tampons, I thought that I should explain to the clerk why I was buying these, too.

"They're not for me," I said. "We're going to use them for padding for a shin guard." "That's OK," she said, "as long as the kid doesn't know what they are intended to be used for." I told her that the kid knows what they are because he's 49 years old! Everyone around laughed.

Jim: After three days on the Erie Canal we began to feel like we'd had enough. After the Oswego River the scenery was pretty boring—like driving through central Ohio, Indiana and Nebraska. The good part was that we met several people who had made the trip to the Bahamas and the West Indies, and they had excellent advice for us. Like the couple from Alpena, Michigan, Mark, who had quit his job as an emergency room physician, and Karen, on leave from her teaching job. Since they were on their way back to Michigan, they gave us their "lucky crab net" as a gift for our stay in the Chesapeake. We spent the evening sharing a bottle of Bahamian rum and talking about their adventures. They had gone to Nova Scotia by way of the St. Lawrence, and the trip had taken them two months. That confirmed that we had made the right decision by choosing the canal route. They had then spent two summers in Nova Scotia before heading for the Bahamas, going pretty much where we hoped to go, from Maine to the Chesapeake and then down the Intracoastal Waterway to Florida and the Bahamas.

There were few towns along the canal, and most of them had no facilities, not even a wall for boats transiting the canal to tie up to. As we pulled into the gas dock of one of the rare marinas, an old codger leaning in a chair up against the tiny marina office said, "Watcha need?"

"Gas, water, ice, and a pumpout," I answered.

"Well, we got 'em all."

He brought out hoses and I filled the gas and water tanks. We had to move the boat up the dock to get to the "honey wagon." Angie and I were pulling it by bow and stern lines, when the boat stopped. "How deep is it here?" I asked.

"Sixteen feet."

We gave another tug on the lines, but she was definitely sitting in mud and wasn't going to move forward. We pulled her back and then finally got her up to the honey wagon by pushing her well out into the canal. That's when you hope that you've secured your lines well on the boat. Instructions for how to use the pumpout came from from the attendant back at his station leaning against the wall of the marina. I stretched the hose out to the dock, jammed the rubber end into the waste outlet and had Angie hold it while I went back over to the wagon and pressed the start button. Nothing happened. A boy came over to help and poked the machine a little, while the attendant yelled some encouragement, "Hold that hose in there tight!" and then left. Finally the attendant ambled back, grumbling "Only one out of ten people can use this equipment right." Apparently he wasn't one of them because he couldn't make it work and we never did get our pumpout.

Taking showers along the canal was a special challenge. As I said, there were no facilities and we had to rely on our two and a half gallon sun shower and take showers in the cockpit. The first time we did this we hung towels on the lifelines, let down the awning flaps and were able to take showers in the nude without a problem. But the next night, at Lock Nine, after we had hung up the towels and let down the flaps, a car came up to a picnic table near the stern of our boat. Mom and Pop unloaded a bunch of little kids and they all began to fish. So much for nude bathing. Angie put on her bathing suit. I hung the shower from the mast, and she began to shower. She is trying to discreetly wash her body and I am changing down below getting ready for my turn to shower, when a couple walk up the pier. She points down into the cockpit and the cabin, while he cranes his neck to get a better look. I retreat to the forepeak to get my swim suit on, muttering "Some people!"

Castleton, New York: Raising the Mast

Just a week after we started down the Erie Canal from Oswego we arrived at Castleon-on-Hudson, where we could step our mast and become a sailboat again. Castleton was a tiny village with a boat club that specialized in masts. That is, they had a gin pole (a kind of hand operated crane for lifting the mast) which they rented for fifteen dollars a shot to sailors exiting or about to enter the canals. You provided all of the labor yourself. I was nervous about us lifting a half ton mast and guiding it through a small hole in the deck, through the cabin, and down to the mast step resting on the keel of the boat. Castleton is right on the Hudson, and the wake from passing boats could be a big problem, but the alternative was to go to Riverview Marina, further down the Hudson, where they charged $135 to do the job. That was pretty close to our budget for a week, so we opted for Castleton. The day we arrived, Saturday, was very windy and there was a lot of boat traffic. We didn't get under the gin pole until 6 p.m. and had just about decided to wait for the early calm of Sunday morning to do the job. One motorboat wake at the wrong time would create havoc. We didn't need an extra hole through our deck. We were just getting stuff like the awning and the boom cleared off the deck when Philippe, a sailor from Montreal who had just pulled two masts on his 57 foot ketch,* came by and offered to help. We jumped at the chance.

Philippe showed us how to find the balance point of the mast so that when we raised it off the cradles we could put it where we wanted it. He handled the winch and directed from there. Very slowly and carefully we hoisted the mast, swung it 180 degrees. and lifted it up. I held the butt down and guided it toward the partners (the hole in the deck that the mast fits through) while Angie and another volunteer held the stays and lines out of the way. Finally the mast was vertical and passed over the partners. We prayed that no motorboats would come by. Local boats slowed as they passed Castleton, but even their wake could mean trouble. A bad wake when the mast was through the deck but not yet stepped could cause havoc in the cabin because of the mast swinging around. No motorboats passed, but as we lowered the mast, I could see that it wouldn't hit the step. We had to move the boat forward, and when we did the mast settled into the step. Philippe left us to secure the mast. He was an excellent teacher. It was not the last time that a sailor from Canada helped us solve a problem.

Chapter Five:

A Sailboat Again

It was a thrill to get our sails up and become a sailboat again. From Castleton we would sail down the Hudson, around the Battery at the tip of Manhattan, up the East River to Long Island Sound and then on the ocean up to Maine. After sailing through the Palisades, passing West Point on the Hudson, we sighted a magnificent large black classic looking sloop sailing upriver. As it passed we recognized it as Pete Seeger's boat *Clearwater* sailing up the river campaigning for a cleaner environment.

New York Harbor

At our last anchorage on the Hudson, we had to get up before the sun to reach the East River before the tide turned against us. The current through the East River runs as high as eight knots, and since our best cruising speed under power was under six, we'd have been swept backwards if we hit it at the wrong time. So we were underway at first light, and arrived at New York Harbor when morning was at its full glory. We'd never seen such a confusion of boat traffic. Ferry boats, ocean liners, tugs with and without barges, power boats of all kinds and sizes all coming seeming to be aiming right at us. By this time Angie was an accomplished helmsman, and she steered while I watched the traffic and tried to determine a safe course through the maze. We made it through the harbor and up the East River without incident, swept long by the favorable current, and by late afternoon we were safely anchored in Oyster Bay on Long Island Sound.

Angie at the helm in the East River, New York City,
with the Twin Towers in the background

Mystic

Angie: A big difference between traveling in 1985 when we made our big trip aboard *Escapade* and traveling today is the absence of ATM machines. No matter where we go today, if we need cash we just find the nearest automatic teller and withdraw money in the local currency. In 1985 we carried travelers' checks. For those of you too young to remember, these were prepaid checks, issued by some major bank such as Western Union, or Cooks of London. In theory they were acceptable like cash anywhere, but in fact it was sometimes difficult to find a place to cash them. In the Bahamas, for example, we spent hours sitting on the floor in the local bank waiting on the one day it was open for our turn to cash some checks. So in addition to travelers checks, we carried a large amount of cash.

Though we never really felt threatened on the boat (well, with the exception of that one time out on the ocean on our way back from the Bahamas—we'll tell that story later), we did occasionally hear stories of unwanted visitors coming aboard. In those days we never locked our boat when we left it—none of the cruising sailors we knew did—but we did think it prudent to put our cash some place where it wouldn't be easily found. It's not easy to find a good hiding place on a small sailboat, so Jim put our bundle into an empty coffee can and tucked it back among our stored provisions.

Before we left Long Island Sound, we decided to pay a visit to Mystic Seaport in Connecticut, a museum dedicated to the whaling industry that once dominated New England. Mystic is home to the *Charles Morgan*, the last surviving whaling ship. We were fascinated by the cramped quarters shared by the whalers, who were sometimes out to sea for five years at a time. I can only imagine the hardships they endured, and Jim cringed at the tiny bunks, no more that five feet long. Men might have been shorter in those days, but still . . . But I'm getting ahead of my story.

Since we were on a tight budget and never went to marinas if we could avoid it, we anchored off Dobson's Boatyard and took a taxi to the seaport. One of my favorite things to do when traveling is to talk to cab drivers, and so I struck up a conversation with this one. He was interested in hearing about the trip we were on. When he heard we were headed for The Bahamas, he asked if we were carrying any weapons. That was a question that came up often. People have an exaggerated opinion of the dangers travelers face because they hear a few horror stories and think those incidents are more common than they are. At least that was true in 1985, although in some ways the world does seem to be a more dangerous place today. Anyway, we had decided against carrying a weapon. There were just as many stories of people being harmed with their own weapons as there were people using them to defend themselves. We knew that if we were confronted by drug runners in the Bahamas, or some such, we would be greatly outgunned. The best strategy would be to submit and give them what they wanted. Besides, you couldn't legally bring a gun into the Bahamas, and if the authorities found one on your boat, the boat would be confiscated. We figured that was a bigger risk, since the boat was our home.

The cab driver agreed. "I've got a friend who goes to the Bahamas every year," he said. "I don't think he locks his boat. And his boat was only entered once when he wasn't there. All they took was his groceries."

Jim and I just looked at each other and laughed. There went the idea that the coffee can was a safe hiding place. We could imagine an astonished thief going through the groceries and coming up with our bankroll. After that, I just kept my cash in my pillow case, where any competent thief would be sure to look for it. I think Jim hid his behind the cassette player. At any rate, we never had any unwelcome guests aboard.

Aye, Aye Capitan!

When you are cruising, things can go from delightful to—well, not so delightful—very quickly. After visiting Jim's brother in New Haven, we had a great sail under spinnaker up Long Island Sound to Niantic. We came into the harbor under sail and picked up a guest mooring. It was a hot and humid day and I was tired, so I lay down for a nap while Jim rowed the dinghy ashore to pay for the mooring. He returned to tell me that it would cost us $10, which seemed like a lot to us on our $25 dollar a day budget. But the dock master had told Jim that we could go up the Niantic River where we could anchor for free.

The river anchorage was close and we thought it would be an easy motor ride, so we let go of our mooring and took off. As I tell the rest of this story, you have to realize that we were on a steep learning curve with respect to tidal currents, coming from the Great Lakes where there are virtually no tides. The tide was falling. That meant we had to fight an adverse current going up the river. We had to negotiate two bridges, the second one a railroad bridge that opened only on a set schedule. As we passed through the first one the current forced *Escapade* to crab dangerously toward some pilings under the bridge. Jim gunned the engine and we escaped that potential disaster, but almost immediately we had to anchor to wait for the second bridge to swing open.

We made it through the second bridge and began following the narrow twisting channel toward the anchorage. I was following the chart and calling off the channel markers as Jim steered. We could see the anchored boats ahead, and Jim saw some markers that weren't on the chart. He thought they were private buoys that marked a more direct route to the anchorage. He said "Let's follow these." I tried to talk him out of it. Well, Jim was the captain, and I followed his orders even if I didn't agree with him. On a boat, one person is in charge and in difficult situations you can't be arguing about what you are going to do. It's that simple. Jim headed *Escapade* up through what he thought was a channel and she came to a sudden stop, stuck hard in the mud. What he had taken for private channel buoys were lobster pot buoys, something else we weren't accustomed to on the Great Lakes.

Jim took out an anchor to the far side of the channel to try to kedge* us off, and we managed to get *Escapade*'s bow swung around in the right direction, but that's as far as we got. Jim winched on the anchor and rocked the boat while I skulled with the tiller, but *Escapade* wouldn't budge. A canoeist came up along side offering to help and we got him to hang off the boom to heel the boat, but that didn't work. A warden came by in a motor boat and suggested that since the tide was falling, we should wait for the rising tide to float the boat free. That probably would have worked, but we didn't want to wait 8 or 10 hours for the tide to lift us, so we kept trying. Then a couple of navy men came up in a motor launch and asked if they could help. Jim threw them the second anchor rode,* passed one end through a bow chock and tied the end around the mast. As the navy men used their powerful motor to haul on the boat, Jim rocked the boat and I skulled. Suddenly there was a loud bang as the line snapped. Fortunately, Jim had a new spare anchor rode. He got that out, and we tried again. This time *Escapade* came free like she had been shot out of a slingshot. I nearly hit a buoy as we came into the channel and had to react quickly to keep us from going aground on the other side. After we made it the rest of the way up the channel and were anchored, we surveyed the boat for damage. The only thing that we could see was that the topping lift, that goes from the top of the mast to the end of the boom, was hung up on a spreader. Jim said I would have to go up the mast to free it. I wasn't very happy, in fact I was seething inside because Jim hadn't listened to me, but I would have gone up the mast if I had to. When living on a boat you do what you have to do. But I asked Jim If we couldn't get it free with the boat hook. He tried that, and it worked.

I went up and sat on the cabin top and was quiet. When living on *Escapade*, if I was angry and unhappy about something I would just remain very quiet. After all, Jim was the captain. (Today, nearly 40 years later, there is nothing quiet about me.) Jim came up and sat beside me. He didn't have to ask what was wrong, he knew. Finally

I blurted out, "I'm never coming back to this place. The only way I would ever come back to this place was if you proposed to me!" I'm not sure why I said that. I certainly wasn't expecting a proposal or a return to the Niantic River, for that matter. Jim went below, and a few minutes later he came back with two gin and tonics. "Will you marry me?" he asked. I began beating on him. "Don't play with my mind," I yelled. "I mean it," he said. "Will you marry me?" I think he was afraid that I was going to jump ship. Many couples do split up when living aboard a boat. This life is not for everyone, and not like you see in the movies. It's a hard, challenging life. You really have to get along and work together. And I love it. After 40 years together we are still working together, writing this book, and enjoying each other's company.

Chapter Six:

Down East to Maine

Jim: John Palmer and Zelda Zabinsky, friends I had made at the University of Michigan Sailing Club, joined *Escapade* in Boston, and we set out from Marblehead for Eastport, Maine, two hundred and fifty miles east. They were great additions to the crew. John was a careful navigator with experience on the Pacific Ocean, and Zelda loved to handle the helm. Zelda is also the luckiest person I have ever known. She denies being a witch even though she was born on October 31, but the breezes alway seemed to spring up when she was at the helm. The first evening out, John and Zelda were on watch. The sea was calm and we were motoring on a gentle swell. Zelda reached down into the cabin for the binoculars. "Think I'll look for whales," she said. Within fifteen minutes she called, "I think I see spouts!" Soon we could see the great humpbacks breaking the surface. John motored over in their direction and three sets of flukes waved at us as the whales dove. When we resumed course we saw several more whales in front of us, closer than the first ones, but still far enough away to cause more thrill than anxiety.

The next night Angie and I, on the midnight watch, were talking about hitting whales. I assured her that whales have excellent navigation equipment and would avoid us. "It would be a dumb whale that would let itself be hit by a sailboat,'" I said. I didn't mention the Baileys, who spent 118 days in a life raft after their boat had been sunk by whales.

We were gliding along with the spinnaker billowing out from the bow, enjoying a fantastic light show. An August meteor shower sent shooting stars across the sky every few seconds. Phosphorescence made light dance on top of the little whitecaps as far as we could see, and the V-shaped wake from the dinghy trailing our stern was a brilliant flame. I heard a door banging down below. When I stood up to go investigate I saw a large black contoured shape in the water just ahead. Angie and I both watched with our hearts pounding in our throats as we glided by. All we could see was a black shape, the absence of phosphorescence. Whatever it was, it was oblong and almost twice the length of our boat. "Could that have been a whale?" We hated to think of how a dozing whale might react if we bumped it. As dawn came, wet saw some huge patches of seaweed floating on the surface of the ocean. Which explains what we'd seen before. At least we hoped so.

After fifty-two hours of near perfect sailing, including the thirteen hour, all night spinnaker run, we ran into a fog bank and decided to stop short at Cutler, Maine. The fog was so dense as we approached the harbor that we couldn't see more than a boat length ahead of us. I was at the helm and Angie stood at the bow listening for the bell buoy that marked the middle of the channel and calling out directions to me. Around us we could hear the murmur of engines of boats that we couldn't see. Suddenly the fog lifted, the sun shone through, and we found ourselves in the harbor. Looking back we saw the submerged rocks that we had barely missed. We were relieved that we made it safely.

Cutler was just short of our goal of Eastport, but stopping there was a lucky circumstance. Cutler is as attractive harbor as you will find anywhere, "the last real working harbor on the coast" as the local storekeeper described it. It is far enough east to be beyond the reach of most cruising sailors and land tourists. It had retained its character as a lobstering village and escaped the economic disaster that had hit Eastport when the herring industry that supported the town disappeared.

It was Saturday when we climbed the long ladder, over twenty feet at low water, to Neil Corbett's dock. We caught Neil just as he was driving into his driveway.

"Want some water, do you?' he greeted us.

"No, we hoped to buy some lobsters."

"Can't sell you any lobsters. Quit work three hours ago. Could give you some water, though." Since there was no place to fill your tanks in Cutler, this was not a senseless offer. We made a date to meet Neil at 7:30 the next morning. Then he dipped us our four handsome lobsters from his live storage cage and we carried them in a bucket of salt water to our next—and their final—destination.

While in Cutler we were lucky to meet George and Marion Emerson from the Fox Islands who were cruising on their beautiful black Alden yawl, Nightwind. Veterans of more than thirty years cruising Maine, they introduced us to several delightful anchorages which we later explored—anchorages like Rogue Island, The Cows Yard, and Perry Creek. Each one had its own special delight, rare birds, a sandy beach, mussel beds where a dinner of perfect mussels could be gathered from the rocks in a few minutes.

From Cutler, a four hour sail with a fair wind and tide brought us to Eastport, the easternmost point in the U.S. Eastport was a big disappointment. Not only was it economically depressed, with the fishing industry dying and little tourism or other viable replacement, but it had no gas. We were happy to leave there and head up Head Harbour Passage for an anchorage in East Quoddy Head Harbour, on Campobello Island. The Passage has a confluence of currents from the Passamaquoddy River, Cobscook Bay, and the Bay of Fundy. As we sailed through the ripples and swirls where the currents met, we passed through swarms of small sandpiper like birds. We later identified these as phalaropes and learned that birders cross continents to set up their telescopes on Campobello Island for a distant view of them.

In 1985 we entered Head Harbour without giving more than a passing thought to the fact that we had crossed an international border between Maine and New Brunswick, Canada. Used almost exclusively by Canadian herring and cod fishermen, Head Harbour is a picturesque place. For two days we rode the elevator of the twenty-six foot tides, rafted to a moored fishing boat. We spent our days hiking the rocky shores, taking photos of stranded fishing boats and tall, mussel encrusted, cross timbered docks, and dining on fresh cod and snow crab legs which we bought from the local fishermen. We felt a strong desire to explore further east, perhaps to St. Johns and on to Nova Scotia, but summer was nearing an end. Reluctantly we cast off our lines and headed west and south.

There were still plenty of delights to savor as we cruised west past Schoodic Point—swimming in the clear cool water off Opeechee Island, musseling, wading the tidal pools looking for starfish and sand dollars, visiting famous ports like Christmas Cove, and Southwest Harbor. By the time we reached Camden, in late August, the weather had turned damp and cold.

Angie and Martha in Maine

At Camden our friend Martha Torrey replaced John and Zelda as crew. We were sorry to see John and Zelda go, for they had made the 230 mile passage to Maine possible, but we couldn't have had a better replacement as a sailing companion than Martha. The Emersons, whom we had met in Cutler, owned a "camp" on Penobscot Bay and had invited us to pick up a mooring in the Fox Islands. It was a lovely spot. Marion, driving us around at breakneck speed in her motor launch, showed us a miniature canyon with a waterfall where she said, "If there were fairies and elves this is where they would live." We were enchanted and stayed a few days, enjoying fine weather and dinners of chowder made with mussels we harvested off the rocks at low tide. From the Fox Islands we cruised on to Falmouth-Foreside in Casco Bay. There, on Labor Day weekend, we were hit with the first real Nor'easter of the fall season. The temperature plummeted and we resorted to heating a brick on the kerosene cook stove to radiate some heat through the cabin. After bobbing on a mooring in the choppy harbor for three days, waiting for a change in the weather, we decided to take the launch ashore for a visit. The dock master at Handy's in Falmouth-Foreside was a crusty downeasterner, typically laconic. On our return trip the wind drove the cold drizzle into us as the dock master boarded the launch with Martha, Angie and me and headed us out toward *Escapade*.

"You'll need a fire today," he said.

"Yeah," I replied. "I'll have to get the brick heating up."

He looked at Martha, Angie, and me with just the trace of a smile. "You're all three on the same brick?" With only one brick to keep us warm and New England fall definitely on the way, we knew it was time to begin our southward migration.

Food

Angie: Food has always been important to me, so when we got to Maine, I was in heaven. We bought fresh fish from the fishermen, lobsters from the lobster agents, both for $3.00 a pound, bought wild blueberries at the local markets, and eventually we harvested fresh mussels ourselves from the rocks at low tide. (I just bought cod at Whole Foods for $13 a pound, and that was on sale!)

Cooking on an alcohol stove, which I had learned to do in the North Channel, was a real challenge. The saying is that on an alcohol stove you can bring cold water to room temperature in about two hours. So Jim had converted the two burner stove to kerosene, but it was still a challenge. We had no oven, so everything had to be cooked stovetop and in as few pans as possible. While sailing in the Canadian North Channel Jim and I had begun writing a cookbook which we called "The Well Flavoured Passage," telling how we put together interesting meals using stuff you could have available on a small boat. We learned how to bake bread and pies in the pressure cooker, using it like a Dutch oven. As long as you have basic ingredients like spices, garlic and onions, along with canned goods, and a little creativity you can muster up some mighty good meals. For instance, in Quoddy Head, where we went after Cutler, we had some left over cod. One day was the limit for keeping anything in our less than reliable ice box. So I cooked pasta with mushrooms, onions, green peppers, zucchini, and spaghetti sauce. I threw in the leftover cod, and what a feast! Back in Cutler, we had lobster paella for dinner.

While in Cutler we made a wonderful discovery. The rocks exposed by the low tide were covered with mussels. Later in the Fox Islands Jim and Martha went out in the dinghy and scraped up a bucket of them. I steamed them with a little water, onions, garlic, tomatoes and some white wine and we had another delicious meal. (I have a wooden paddle hanging by the stove inscribed "I love cooking with wine. Sometimes I even put it in the food!")

Chapter Seven:

On Down the Coast

Jim: After Martha left us in Falmouth, we enjoyed a largely uneventful pleasure sail from Portland down to Provincetown, Cape Cod, with a stop at Hadley Harbor on Cape Cod. As we entered the harbor we were greeted by a doe with two fawns. From there through the Cape Cod Canal to Marion, Mass. In Marion we were to be joined by Mike Carter, who would help us sail *Escapade* mostly off shore to New Jersey. Mike, now a professor at Dartmouth, was another sailor I knew from the U of M Sailing Club and an expert addition to our crew. Mike would later help us to sail *Escapade* back from the Bahamas and be involved in our high seas encounter with drug traffickers.

We had a day layover in Marion, while we waited for Mike to arrive. We found ourselves docked next to another Tartan 30, almost identical to ours, named *Escappa*. Angie was swabbing the deck and struck up a conversation with Rocky Keith, the owner of *Escappa*. Angie called me up and we were soon in a conversation about our boats. Since we were there for a day, Rocky wondered if we would be interested in a daysail. He said he seldom could find crew who knew their way around a boat and we were happy to go with him. Rocky was glad to have someone aboard who "knew the ropes." Afterwards, he invited us to dinner with his family at their "cottage" on Converse Point (their winter home was also in Marion, a few miles away). Without any notice, Mrs. Keith generously stretched the dinner of swordfish steak, baked potato, green beans, potato salad, and blueberry confit to accommodate a couple of itinerant sailors along with a flock of family members. Angie felt that she was underdressed for such a gourmet meal in an elegant setting.

After our daysail on *Escappa* and our fine dinner with the Keiths, we left Marion with Mike aboard and headed for Block Island, RI. Mike and I had both been small boat racers and we could never resist a bit of competition, and Angie is as competitive as anyone. So as we approached Block Island, we noticed a Pearson 36 on a parallel course with us. Angie was steering and Mike was tending the sheets on a close reach. While I was lounging, sitting on the cabin top, I noticed the crew on the Pearson eyeing us.

"Listen," I practically whispered to Mike and Angie, "they're trying to get ahead of us. Don't look at them, just listen to me and do what I say." Then I quietly told Angie when to head up or bear off, and Mike to trim or ease the sails, calling on all my experience racing on Base Line Lake in light and shifting winds. For a moment the Pearson, sailing a steady course, was gaining on us. "It ain't over until it's over," Mike said, quoting Casey Stengel. We kept watching the wind shifts and carefully adjusting our sails. Slowly we pulled ahead of the Pearson and sailed into Great Salt Pond ahead of them. Then we gave them a show by anchoring under sail.

Since we had an extra hand on deck and a favorable weather forecast, we decided to bypass Long Island Sound and New York Harbor and take a straight shot from Block Island to Atlantic City. This would be another multiple day passage. We didn't have the reliable long range weather forecasts that we have today, but we set off in fine weather, with blue skies, puffy white clouds and a favorable wind that allowed us to reach along at a steady five knots. When we were doing overnighters with an extra person aboard, we set up watches with one person on duty for three hour shifts during the day time, and two for a longer watch during the night. Of course, as captain, I was always on call. One night, in the Gulf of Maine with Martha aboard, I had been sleeping while Martha and Angie were on watch. The wind was light and Martha and Angie were relaxed in the cockpit. I should point out that Martha and Angie are both great conversationalists, while I tend to be on the quiet side. Anyway, I woke feeling something different about the motion of the boat. I came on deck to find *Escapade* hove to* after having quietly come about without Angie and Martha noticing. We all laughed about that and I have to say that from that point on everyone's first attention was on the boat. Both Martha and Angie were excellent crew members.

On this leg, we were glad to have Mike along. The winds were favorable, but light for the first leg passing Long Island and across New York Harbor, and we were forced to use the "Iron Jenny" off and on to keep up our five knot average speed. Then at eight o'clock we were hit with a storm and were running in 15 to 20 knot winds out of the north under a double reefed* mainsail alone. After the storm we motorsailed* in shifty winds until about one in the morning, when the wind came up strong from the northeast. Angie and I were on watch. Our course was directly downwind, so sailed wing and wing with the smaller of our two genoas poled out to starboard and our reefed mainsail out to port. The following waves were three to six feet, giving us the ride of our lives. We frequently found ourselves surfing down the waves that rose up behind us. Surfing, the knot meter read over seven and a half knots, a speed theoretically impossible for our boat. We could see the lights of a tug pulling a barge off to starboard. The swells were so large that the lights kept appearing and disappearing, and each time they appeared, we studied them to see if we were on a converging course. Sailing wing and wing as we were, we had very little leeway on our course. If we got a little off, our jenny would backwind and we would be in serious trouble. The waves made steering difficult, and we needed two hands on the tiller to keep *Escapade* on a steady path. Fortunately the tug and barge, maintaining about the same speed as we were, never got any closer. The winds and waves continued through the night and the next day until about four o'clock in the afternoon, when we finally had to turn the engine on. At 1715 nautical time (a quarter after five in the afternoon) we picked up a mooring in the City Marina at Atlantic City. Our logbook noted "What a Sail!"

Mike Carter left *Escapade* in Atlantic City. We were sorry to see him go, but he assured us that he would be available to help us bring the boat back from the Bahamas when we were ready to do that. He had been a great help in the long passage from Block Island to Atlantic City, and like Zelda, John and Martha, welcome companionship as we explored the East Coast. From now on we would be working our way down the Intracoastal Waterway, and overnight passages would end for the duration.

Angie: We did have one interesting experience in Atlantic City. After Mike left, we were having breakfast in one of the casinos before heading for the Chesapeake and Delaware Canal and Chesapeake Bay. Now *Escapade* had no refrigeration other than an ice box, and because it was often a hassle to get ice, we tried to do without it as much as possible. This presented few problems, but I enjoyed milk or cream in my morning coffee, and milk doesn't keep very well without refrigeration. So when the waiter put a bowl full of those little containers of half and half on the table, I slipped most of them into my handbag. On his next round, the waiter noticed the empty bowl and immediately replaced it with a full one. Well, I thought why not, and I scooped up those as well. The waiter then replaced it with another bowl. He either thought we used an awful lot of cream in our coffee, or, more likely, was curious to see just how many of the little creamers we would take. After we returned home, I pulled the same stunt in our local vegetarian restaurant. As I was paying the bill the cashier noticed the cream in my purse and commented, "Oh, cream to go?"

Chapter Eight:

Chesapeake Bay

From Atlantic City we headed down to Cape May and then by way of the Chesapeake and Delaware Canal to Chesapeake Bay. We spent the better part of October in the Chesapeake, long enough to fall in love with the area. Along with the North Channel of Lake Huron and the coast of Maine, it became one of our favorite cruising grounds, but our first days there were not all roses. For one thing, we found that running aground was a constant worry. Running aground in the Chesapeake was not the catastrophe that it would have been in the North Channel, where the bottom is generally rocky. The bottom here was soft silt. The problem was that many areas were shallow and the silt shifted with the tides, so that you could never quite rely on the charts. After a couple of groundings we noticed that we were getting a little bit of water in our bilge, apparently seeping in where the strong keel bolts fastened our lead keel to the hull of the boat.

Our friend Mike Sepanski, who had sailed with Jim on Lake Superior and who had originally been going to sail with Jim on this cruise, lived in Baltimore. We had been using him as our mail drop (remember, no internet and no cell phones in 1985) and were looking forward to connecting with him when we got to Baltimore. We figured that when we got there we would have the boat hauled, get the keel bolts tightened, the bottom cleaned and painted, and any other problems that we might discover taken care of. As it happened, we had to be towed into Baltimore. The shift cable froze up and we couldn't operate the engine. We contacted Mike and he enlisted his friend and sailing partner Sue Fortney to meet us with her power boat and tow us into the marina.

While we were in Baltimore we had our first brush with a hurricane. Hurricane Gloria was working her way up the coast, and while she wasn't expected to make a direct hit on Baltimore, everyone was worried about the super high tides that she might cause. At first we thought we would stay aboard *Escapade* to take care of her, but discretion won out and after securing her with extra lines, we went to stay with Mike. (After seeing the devastation that hurricanes caused in other coastal communities, we knew we had made the right choice.) It was a night of great anxiety as we followed the path of the hurricane. There were heavy rains, but Gloria came and went with no damage to *Escapade*.

We ended up staying with Mike two weeks while *Escapade* was being worked on, and spent $780 out of our reserve kitty. We thought that was an exorbitant amount. (It would have been about $1800, just under two BOAT units,* in today's dollars.) Maintenance included getting the keel bolts tightened, the seam where the keel met the hull recaulked, a new control for the shift and gas, and the outboard cleaned and tuned. While the boat was hauled for this work, we noticed a notch about the thickness of a man's thumb on the trailing edge of the keel. We couldn't figure out how we could have hit something going in reverse hard enough to gouge out the lead. That mystery was solved later near the marine base at Camp Lejeune. On the bright side, we got to attend the Annapolis Sailboat Show. One boat that caught our fancy was the new Tayana 37, a boat built along classic lines and intended for serious ocean sailing. We dreamed of someday continuing our sailing adventures trading *Escapade*, designed for Great Lakes and bay sailing, for a boat like that. If we could have afforded to we would have traded right then, but the Tayana, at $100,000, was way out of our price range.

Once we had all of the maintenance completed on *Escapade*, we had ample time to explore the bay. Our insurance wouldn't allow us to go south of Norfolk, Virginia, until after November 1, the official end of the hurricane season. (Hurricane Kate, which we met up with in Charleston on November 22, evidently didn't get the memo.) October turned out to be a beautiful time to discover the delights of the Chesapeake's Eastern Shore. First there were the towns of Oxford and St. Michaels that took us back to earlier days. Oxford was the quieter of the two, and was to become important to us when we revisited the Chesapeake on *Bel Canto*. St. Michaels was busy with visiting sailors from Baltimore and Annapolis, mainly because of the museum there that heralded the early days of life on the bay. There we saw the skipjacks, beautiful shallow draft sailing vessels that had been used to dredge for oysters. But the greatest delights came in the little anchorages tucked away up the rivers and creeks that mark the Eastern Shore. One of our favorites (and one we revisited on *Bel Canto* many years later) was Dividing Creek up the Wye River. We were alone and sat in the cockpit enjoying the silence while watching the blue herons fishing along the shore, then eating our dinner of blue crabs in the cockpit under a star filled sky. It was moments like this that drew us back to the sea many years later.

Food 2

Angie: We had read the book *Beautiful Swimmers* that described the blue crabs, for which the Chesapeake is famous, and the watermen who made their living harvesting them. When we found our way into Tighlman Creek, a tiny anchorage on the Eastern Shore, we met one of the watermen, who was just setting out to do some crabbing. He said that very few cruisers found their way into the creek, and he was happy to spend some time chatting with us. He had read both *Beautiful Swimmers* and James Michener's *Chesapeake*. He described how difficult the life of a waterman was, especially as you grow older, but he still enjoyed it and loved being outdoors. He was sorry that his son was not following in his footsteps, but said he understood that he was part of a dying breed. He divulged to us the watermen's secret for catching blue crabs. "Everyone says you use chicken necks," he said, "but eels work a whole lot better," and he gave us a whole bunch of eels to use for bait. The blue crabs are beautiful creatures. He told us how to distinguish the females, or sooks, by their red painted "fingernails" or claws and the apron on their belly. On the immature females, which you did not want to eat because they haven't molted, it was V shaped. So Jim tied the eels to some whipping line, and soon we were enjoying crab dinners whenever we wanted. When we cooked them in boiling water they turned bright red. Old Bay seasoning was the only spice needed to bring out the full flavor. One of my greatest disappointments when we were back in the Chesapeake on *Bel Canto*, was that *Bel Canto*, with her six foot draft, couldn't make it past the bar at the entrance of Tighlman Creek.

And then there were the oysters. At that time you could still see the oystermen standing in their boats with the long handled tongs that they used for scraping oysters off the bottom. As you can imagine, these men all had powerful shoulders. They would sometimes anchor their boats near the entrance to harbors and offer their oysters to sailboats entering or leaving. On our second trip to the Chesapeake, thirty years later, these boats and the way of life they represented had disappeared. It's no wonder. Talk about a hard way to make a living!

Tonging for Oysters

Before we left the Chesapeake, we wanted to visit Smith Island. Smith Island lies down near the Virginia border in the Chesapeake and is slowly sinking into the water. At one time Smith Island was an almost totally isolated community, and when we visited there on *Escapade*, it was still pretty insular. As we approached through the narrow channel, some watermen anchored off a ways to the side held our some oysters offering to sell them to us fresh from the boat, but Jim was afraid of going aground if he left the shallow channel, so we passed by. But then, before we had reached the small harbor, we were attacked by swarms of biting flies. I tried to keep them off Jim with a flyswatter while he struggled to keep the boat in the channel, but finally we made it in and were tied up to the dock. We were eager to visit Mrs. Kitching's Kitchen, legendary among cruising sailors. Mrs. Kitching offered meals in her home, by reservation only, to visiting boaters. She was a very friendly person and sat at the table and chatted with everyone. She emphatically informed us that her place was not a restaurant. "People don't order what they want here, they get what I serve them!" The meal we got that day started with crab chowder, followed by crab cakes, ham, creamed corn, potatoes, jello salad, green beans, home made bread, candied apples, and cheese cake. All of this for nine dollars a person and worth every penny!

Chapter Nine:

Norfolk and the Intracoastal Waterway

From Smith Island we worked our way down to Norfolk where we would begin our nearly eleven hundred mile trek down the inland waterway to West Palm Beach. This is where we planned to cross the Gulf Stream to the Bahamas. Waiting for a break in the early winter weather, we ended up at Waterside Marina in Norfolk. The following letter to Hope Carlton tells the highlight of our stay there.

[Letter to Hope Carlton, model, actress, and entrepreneur]

June 2, 2016

Dear Ms. Carlton,

The first day of November 1985 was miserably cold. We were at the Waterside Marina in our sailboat *Escapade*, waiting for the weather to improve so that we could continue our trip down the Intracoastal Waterway. A dixieland band that we had heard before and enjoyed listening to was playing at a waterside bar called Philipe's, so we headed there. Rather late in the evening we were joined at our table by two young people who introduced themselves as Tony and Hope. We liked them immediately and had a very enjoyable conversation. Hope, a bubbling 19 year old, was very interested in the fact that this middle aged couple had taken leave from their jobs and embarked on this yearlong adventure. Tony told us that he was electronics salesman in town for a video convention and had just met Hope. When we asked Hope what she did, she simply said. "I'm a model." Tony quickly let us know that Hope Carlton was not "just" a model but July 1985 Playmate of the month. The sweatshirt you were wearing that said "University of Playboy," should have tipped us off, but honestly, Hope, your behavior and dress were so modest that we didn't have a clue. Among other things you told us that you hoped to become very rich and to have a daughter named Charity, since your grandmother's name was Faith.

We spent a very pleasant hour or so together. You gave us your card and invited us to visit you at the convention the next day, where you would be at the Playboy booth. The next morning we left our boat early and visited several magazine shops, sorting through stacks of old Playboy magazines looking for the July 1985 issue. Of course, Norfolk being a Navy town, the sailors, knowing you would be at the convention, had scarfed up every copy. When we got to the convention hall, we found a long line of young men, centerfold posters in hand, waiting for your arrival. Angie was the only female in the line as we joined it to wait for you. We wondered how long we would have to wait to get to you, but when you walked in, transformed in your grey knit suit and pink blouse and in full make up, you saw us, called us to the front of the line, and gave us big hugs. When we told you about our fruitless search for a centerfold, you promised to send us one. You would send it to my 76 year old mother, who lived in Florida and would be our next mail drop.

We weren't sure that you would remember, but when we arrived in Titusville, Florida, Jim's mother delivered our mail and there was the brown envelope containing the July issue with the centerfold inscribed, "Best Wishes to Jim and Angie, Love, Hope Carlton." We proudly attached the poster to the bulkhead of *Escapade*, where it stayed for the rest of our trip. When we entered the Bahamas, it drew the attention of the customs and immigration officer, a tall, good looking Bahamian dressed in an expensive suit and wearing some expensive jewelry including a Rolex watch. As he sat at our dinette with us while we filled out the necessary forms, his eye kept going off to the poster. When we finished, he just said "Some Picture!" I think he hoped we would make him a gift, but we weren't going to give it up.

The other evening we were telling a friend this story, when we decided to google Hope Carlton to see if we could find out what had become of you. To our surprise, we found quite a bit, including that you have had some success as an actress and much as a model, that you had been married to a multi-millionaire with whom you had built up a very successful cosmetic business, and that you have a daughter (we don't know if you named her Charity). You are now the age that Jim was when we met (if you do the math you will realize that he is now 80!) and it sounds like you are at a very good place in your life. We also have a very good life. We spent years whitewater and wilderness canoeing, traveling by van throughout Canada, Mexico, and the United States, and recently spending another year living aboard a sailboat on the East Coast. We have a very rich life, to which our brief acquaintance with you added an interesting bit of color. We wish you the very best!

With love,
Jim and Angie George

We had hoped that we might get a response and hear how this former Playboy Playmate was enjoying middle age, but that didn't happen.

On the Magenta Line

[On charts of the Intracoastal Waterway, the route deemed safe for navigation by small boats is marked with a magenta line.]

Mile one of the Intracoastal Waterway starts on the Elizabeth River at Norfolk, or more properly, Portsmouth just across the river, and it stretches 1240 miles through Virginia, North Carolina, South Carolina, Georgia, and Florida all of the way to Key West. Maybe because we heard it called "the ditch," our initial conception of the ICW was of a more or less straight channel running down the Eastern Seaboard, the mainland on one side and a neat row of offshore islands on the other. To our delight, we found the Intracoastal Waterway to be full of variety. It winds through cedar swamps and savannahs (salt water marshes), follows twisty rivers upstream and downstream, jumping from one to another by short cuts or canals, crosses sounds made by river mouths, flirts with the ocean, then cuts far inland, following long, straight canals to the next river system. For the most part, the water is tidal. The regular surging of the ocean causes currents up to 5 knots and variations in water levels up to eight feet. In places though, the water is nearly fresh, but dyed a deep brown by the roots of trees. Far from being a simple water highway, it presents all kinds of challenges, including shifting sand bars, currents, and changes in depth due to wind and tides.

The Dismal Swamp Canal

From the ICW we got a unique "back door" look at the Eastern Seaboard. We saw country which, because it cannot be easily utilized for commercial purposes, retains its natural beauty, and small towns, historically tied to the sea, where some of the flavor of a way of life hundreds of years ago remains. Because *Escapade* drew* only five feet, we were able to take a shortcut on the waterway through the Dismal Swamp, by way of the Dismal Swamp Canal. The Dismal Swamp was an area of Virginia first surveyed by George Washington, who saw a canal there as being an important connection between Virginia and the colonies to the south. During his term as president slaves were put to work digging the ditch, which was finally finished just after the turn of the 19th century. Later the area became a refuge for runaway slaves and an important route on the Underground Railroad.

From the Elizabeth River Deep Creek Lock took us up twelve feet and we found ourselves in a channel so narrow that it would have been difficult to turn around, stretching in a long straight line through what looked like dense jungle. There was nothing dismal about the Dismal Swamp Canal route. In fact, it took us through one of the most beautiful parts of our trip down the waterway because it was relatively unspoiled. It was possible to feel, as you passed the cypress trees with their hanging vines, that you were in a prehistoric world. The mast occasionally brushed the canopy over the canal, and occasionally we felt a bump as *Escapade* passed a shallow spot. We stayed close to the center of the channel to avoid both the branches overhead and snags hidden in the amber colored water. Depths in the canal were supposed to average about eight to nine feet, but in one spot the depth sounder dipped below five. We scraped, slowed, then pushed through. The boat following us stuck, dragged herself off and turned back.

Our first night on the canal brought us to South Mills, a village adjacent to the second lock, where boats are lowered to the Pasquotank River, which meanders through more cypress swamp to Elizabeth City, North Carolina. The next day was cold and rainy, with storms predicted along the coast, so we decided to lay over for a day. A walk through South Mills revealed a pool hall selling cigarettes and beer, a street rod club meeting, and a black church where some powerful preaching was spilling out onto the street. The following day we motored on down to the very welcoming, picturesque and historic town Elizabeth City. This was a part of our journey that we could not hope to duplicate on *Bel Canto,* with her six foot draft* and 64 foot mast.

On Down the Waterway

There was very little traffic on the Dismal Swamp Canal. In fact, the only other boats we saw on the Dismal Swamp Canal passed us while we were tied to the wall at South Mills. Once we rejoined the main route, however, after crossing Albemarle Sound, we learned what ICW traffic could be like. About eight to ten thousand boats use the Intracoastal Waterway every year. Many of these are local boats, vacationers as well as commercial fishermen. A sizable proportion, though, are "migratory birds," boats from New England, the Chesapeake, and the Great Lakes, making their way south for the winter. Among these, the sailors and the powerboats regard each other like cattlemen and sheepherders. Powerboaters dislike sailors because they seem to hog the middle of the channel, impeding their progress. Sailors dislike powerboats because of their wake. As sailors, we often found ourselves cursing and shaking our fists at some sports fisherman who passed too close, too fast, his wake rocking us, sending pans and dishes flying around the cabin. He was doubtless cursing us for failing to get over to the edge of the channel, perhaps not realizing that with our deep draft, we didn't dare stray too far from the middle.

As a matter of fact, peaceful accommodation between power boaters and sailors is possible. We found that if we slowed to full idle, signaling the overtaking boat that we had done so, and that if he also slowed to a bare crawl, his passing would be painless. The professional crews on the large cruisers most often honored our request for a slow passing. Too often, though, ignorance or lack of common courtesy caused rocky going. The wake of a speeding powerboat would churn up the waterway for minutes after it passed. On the other hand, there are times when sailors welcome the wake of a powerboat. More than one sailor who has come too close to the edge of the channel and gotten stuck has signaled an approaching powerboat to pass at full throttle, then used the wake to break free of the mud.

Some of the sounds we crossed were choked with shrimp boats. One of the worst was St. Simon's Sound where the waterway had just been rerouted and our charts didn't show the proper location of the buoys. On top of this, there was a twenty-five knot wind blowing. As we searched for the next waterway markers, we had to dodge what seemed like hundreds of shrimp boats, wheeling in patterns incomprehensible to us, their "arms" outstretched dragging their nets, ready to take down our rigging if we got in their way. I'm sure the shrimpers were cursing those crazy sailors who didn't seem to know where they were going. To top it all off, the cut from the sound to the next stretch of waterway was blocked by a huge dredge. Angie was at the tiller and decided to just head for the dredge. That turned out to be the way out of the sound. We heaved a sigh of relief when we got clear of that mess.

Shrimp boat coming! Was he trying to intimidate us?

Angie: Dolphin watching was one of our favorite activities on the waterway. After seeing a dolphin and sea lion show in the Boston Aquarium, we fell in love with these intelligent and fun loving creatures. Seeing them free and in their own element, feeding along the edge of a saltwater marsh where we anchored for the night, or frolicking in the wake of a boat on the waterway was even better. They appeared most often near inlets, mostly in pairs, but sometimes alone or in groups. Once we saw several young dolphins playing and having such a good time that they reminded us of a schoolyard full of children out for recess. We also imagined their parents sending them away to play while the old folks enjoyed some solitude.

The dolphins would often swim up to the bow of the boat or alongside, and I would quickly run up on the bow to watch them or try to take photos of them. If I was steering, I'd sometimes get so excited watching them that I'd end up in shallow water. Just outside Marineland, we saw three dolphins coming lickety-split from the direction of the aquarium. We fantasized that they were escapees.

We were also fascinated by the birds we saw along the waterway. Egrets and pelicans, ospreys, and even one bald eagle (a first for both of us). Perhaps the most awe inspiring was the V-formation of giant white swans we saw soaring overhead.

Anchor Hangups

Jim: I stared at the anchor line in dismay. Instead of stretching off the bow as it should, the 3/4" nylon rode* angled tight against the hull, running back to the gap between the fin keel and the skeg* and off from the other side of the boat. A breeze opposed to the current kept the boat perfectly balanced broadside to the current.

I'd noticed how swift the current was a few minutes earlier. We were heading south in the Intracoastal Waterway, just north of Camp LaJeune, North Carolina. A cluster of boats coming into view ahead was our first warning of something unusual. We passed several of them before we saw the runabout with the two marines aboard anchored in the middle of the channel. They signaled us that the waterway was closed ahead. Shelling practice. It would reopen briefly in a half hour. As we turned across the stern of one of the boats anchored and waiting for the reopening, I noted with alarm how quickly we were being borne down toward the bow of the next boat down current. We squeaked by her bowsprit and headed up the line of boats, looking for a spot to drop our hook.

Back at the end of the line we dropped and set our Danforth anchor. Then I watched with almost amused curiosity as the breeze pushed us upstream against the current. Twenty years of sailing on the Great Lakes had not prepared us for all the vagaries of tide and current. I was constantly learning about the behavior of *Escapade*, a Tartan 30 designed for lake sailing, in these conditions. The boat seemed to stabilize, and Angie and I sat down on the cabin trunk to wait for the waterway to reopen. A couple of our traveling companions caught up with us, and we told them about the delay. They anchored further up the waterway. We took some photos and watched the waterfowl, listening to the booming of artillery in the distance and thinking how incongruous that sound was with the peaceful natural beauty around us.

The voice of a bullhorn from the marine runabout wakened us from our revery. The waterway was reopening for 30 minutes, then would be closed for twenty-four hours. I went forward to pull the anchor and discovered the situation described above. I reached down to test the anchor rode. It felt like a steel rod against the hull. I couldn't budge it. The swift current created a huge whirlpool on the downcurrent side of our hull. I started the engine, then quickly turned it off without putting the boat in gear. I wasn't sure that the anchor line wasn't hung up on the prop shaft. If it became twisted around the prop shaft our situation would be dire.

Perplexed, I started to rehearse with Angie ways we might get out of this fix. None of them seemed feasible. Meanwhile, the other boats had pulled anchor and were departing, hurrying to clear the firing rounds before the waterway closed again.

"A buoy on the anchor would be helpful," Angie suggested.

"Yeah," I answered, barely concealing my angry frustration. "A trip line* would be great, only I didn't put one on before we dropped anchor." Then the light dawned.

I pulled all the extra rode from the anchor locker, coiled it and tied the coil to a fender* to use as a buoy.

"Get ready to start the engine," I called to Angie. "I hope this works." I uncleated the anchor rode and threw the whole business overboard, calculating where it had the best chance of clearing the hull. I prayed that we would drift free. A moment later the buoy popped up on the upcurrent side of the hull. We started the engine and came around to retrieve our anchor.

As Angie brought the boat up to the fender we were using as a buoy, I grabbed for it with a boat hook. Our troubles weren't over. I hauled on the anchor, but couldn't retrieve it. It was snagged on something on the bottom. Our 30 minutes were almost up and the marines came up in their launch to see why we were delayed. I told them our dilemma and they took the rode, secured it to their launch, and revved up. The Danforth came up with a bent fluke, and they gave it to us.

"Can I give you something for your trouble?" I called to them.

"Do you have any cigarettes?" they replied.

"Sorry," I said," we don't smoke, but I can give you a beer."

"That'll be great," they replied, so we tossed them a couple of cans of beer, then with great relief headed down the waterway.

It was a long time before we understood what had happened and why, but that incident explained another mystery. When we had the boat hauled in the Chesapeake we'd found a notch about the size of a man's thumb in the trailing edge of the keel, where the lead had been torn sideways. I couldn't figure out how we could have hit something at that angle, but now I realized that the notch had been made by the anchor rode.

After bringing *Escapade* to the ocean from the Great Lakes, we were learning step by step to deal with salt water, tides, and currents. All the reading we had done hadn't prepared us for all the eventualities, and we learned many lessons at the hand of experience. Up to this time, though, none as serious as this one. Worse was to come, and it was due to a peculiarity of fin keeled boats, designed more for racing than for serious cruising. We talked with many other sailors about our problem at Camp LaJeune, but no one had any explanation or advice. Of course, most of them had boats with full keels, or anchored with all chain, or both. Before we solved the mystery we had an incident where we could have lost *Escapade*.

Charleston Harbor

Jim: We arrived in Charleston, South Carolina, in the early afternoon and anchored in the harbor opposite the municipal marina. Hurricane Kate menaced the coast of Louisiana, but we enjoyed fine weather. After carefully setting our plow anchor* and putting *Escapade* in order, we dinghied to the dock and went for a stroll through the beautiful old city. After a couple of hours browsing in shops and gazing at historic buildings, I felt a strong compulsion to get back to the boat. I almost ran, pulling Angie along with me. As soon as we had the anchorage in view, my eye swept the harbor looking for *Escapade*. There she was, but something was wrong. While all of the other boats at anchor pointed east, she pointed west. A knot of fear formed in my chest.

I ran out to the dock and jumped in the dinghy, leaving Angie talking with friends at the dock. As I motored out to *Escapade*, I noticed a small chop forming on the harbor, flinging a splash of spray in my face from time to time. I ignored it, puzzling over *Escapade's* strange attitude. I hoped that maybe she was just in a counter current, or that being of light displacement and moderate fin keel, she was reacting to a change in the tidal current which had just taken place at a different pace from the boats around her. Once aboard, I quickly saw that we were not so lucky and that my fears were justified. *Escapade* was hung up on her anchor line again. I got back into the dinghy and tried pulling the bow and stern around, but the force of the current was too strong to overcome, at least with our little 2 horsepower outboard.

An hour of fruitless effort had passed when I turned on the VHF radio. The weather report was ominous. Kate had turned toward the Florida coast and was crossing the Panhandle. Back on channel 16 I heard *Escapade* being paged. Angie, worried because I had not returned immediately, had asked our friends at the dock to call. I told her the fix we were in and said I couldn't leave *Escapade* to pick her up.

I sat on the cabin trunk thinking about what to do next. The wind and the current were both stronger now, and they opposed each other. There was a nasty chop on the water. The early winter darkness had dropped like a curtain around us. I had already begun getting out a second anchor and anchor rode when Angie arrived aboard a planing Zodiac. Both she and the sailing friend that she had found to bring her out to *Escapade* were life jacketed and drenched from the trip. Once Angie had changed into dry clothes, we got busy. I piled our eighteen pound Danforth and 150 feet of rode into the dinghy, took it out, upcurrent and at an angle to our plow, as far from the boat as I could get and dropped it. Once I was back aboard *Escapade*, we worked the rode back from the bow to our sheet winch in the cockpit and began winching it in. With great relief I felt the Danforth dig into the bottom. It took all my strength to turn the winch, but finally quarter inch by quarter inch we had taken up enough to put some slack in our primary anchor line.

We spent a long time trying to work that line free of the hull. It was at that point that I realized that the rode definitely passed between the hull and the skeg,* and not behind the rudder. I was in the water trying to push the line down under the skeg with a boat hook when I realized that the strong current was frustrating all of my efforts. We finally got it to go under the skeg by tying a lead weight to the line.

The two anchors were not ideally positioned—I would have preferred to have them 180 degrees apart to react to changes in tide and wind direction—but they were both well set and I didn't dare to move them. Conditions were worsening rapidly. The VHF reported that Hurricane Kate had crossed the Florida Panhandle and was headed inland. She had also been downgraded to Tropical Storm Kate. (We received no further word on her progress that night, presumably because the storm had gone inland and was no longer considered a threat to navigation.) I lashed the two anchor rodes together and let out enough line so that the dual rode could easily clear our keel when the tide changed. We had about 200 feet on one rode and close to 150 feet on the other.

We spent the night anxiously watching the anchors and the worsening storm conditions. I was especially worried about what would happen when the tidal current reversed, first at about midnight and then again about six o'clock in the morning. It seemed clear that when the tidal current went slack and released the hull, the wind was free to drive the bow downwind, and then *Escapade* could drift across the slack anchor rode and hang up on it. At each tide change I was standing on deck anxiously watching. It was probably fortunate that the wind was as strong as it was (around 30 knots), because it kept the anchor line taut and the stern off the wind during the tide changes.

Around eight o'clock in the morning we got our next report on Tropical Storm Kate. She was headed right for Charleston Harbor with winds from 50 to 80 miles an hour. Waves in the harbor were four and five feet high. Angie, who had been trying to rest below, began feeling seasick and joined me in the cockpit, where we sat watching the progress of the storm. We could occasionally hear objects bouncing around in the cabin below as the boat pitched and rolled. As the wind increased, I felt an anchor move, and then catch again. I noticed that we were being blown in such a way that if the anchor holding us pulled out, our other anchor rode would likely cross the anchor line of the boat downwind of us (a beautiful little Tahiti ketch). If we dragged, we could take two or three other boats with us. Further downwind was a very solid bridge.

That morning, thank the gods that look after sailors, our anchors held. The wind peaked at 82 miles an hour, turning the sea and the horizon to a blur of gray spray before the eye of the storm passed and the wind shifted. I knew that if we had not been able to get *Escapade* free from her anchor rode before the storm hit, or if she had hung up again, all would have been lost.

Angie: I was really looking forward to exploring this historic city. Since Charleston is a large city, we explored only a small part before sunset. Suddenly Jim sensed that he should return to *Escapade*. We practically ran through the streets to get back to the marina, where we'd left the dinghy tied to a friend's boat. Back at the marina we ran into some of the boaters we'd met along the way, and being the gregarious person I am, I wanted to chat. So I stayed ashore while Jim jumped into the dinghy and headed out to check on *Escapade*.

After a while I realized that Jim was taking a long time to return and I started to worry. The wind had piped up and I knew that something was wrong. I tried to call Jim on our friend's VHF radio but got no response. Finally we connected and Jim told me what I didn't want to hear—that the boat was hung up on the anchor line and he couldn't leave to pick me up.

From past experience I knew that it would take two of us to solve the problem. I had to find someone to take me out to *Escapade*, someone who had a planing dingy with a powerful motor. The wind was still increasing and there was a formidable chop on the bay. Tom, a friend we'd met earlier, agreed to take me. Halfway there, as the spray from the chop hit us in the face, he said that if he could see, he probably wouldn't be out there in his dinghy.

By the time we got to *Escapade*, Jim was already loading a second anchor and piling anchor rode into the dinghy. Winching up on the second anchor, we managed to take the strain off the line wrapped around our keel. While we worked to get it free, the skipper on the boat next to us complained that we were too close. Jim snapped that we would move as soon as we could. Altogether it took us three hours to get *Escapade* free and resting more or less peacefully on two anchors. We sat down and drank a stiff bourbon.

We didn't sleep much that night. The winds kept growing stronger. *Escapade* was straining on her anchor line and pitching and rolling on the waves. Tropical Storm Kate was predicted to hit Charleston about 10 a.m. We sat and waited, ears glued to the VHF. The rain started. Visibility got so bad that we could barely see the other boats in the anchorage. The boat sailed on her anchors and pitched as though we were on the high seas. Loose objects flew around the cabin. The nearby shoreline disappeared. Jim put on his life jacket and crawled out on the deck to check the anchors, then returned to the cockpit and watched the five foot waves roll by. In the cabin I was beginning to feel seasick, so I joined him in the cockpit. I watched the masts in the marina bobbing and wished I were ashore on solid ground. For the first time on the boat I was afraid.

The shore and the other boats disappeared as a tremendous blast of wind turned the world white. Then gradually the wind lessened. I couldn't believe it; our anchors were still holding. We watched the Coast Guard rescuing several boats that had broken loose, while on shore men were working to salvage sections of the dock that had been destroyed. I knew being anchored was safer than being moored at the dock, but I didn't feel safe. I realized that we could die out here. The eye of the storm passed, and though the Coast Guard warned that the second half could be just as bad, it wasn't. The wind shifted so that we were protected by a windward shore and dropped to about thirty knots. We were relieved and thankful that we had made it through. If we would have dragged the anchor there would have been no way of controlling the boat even with the engine on in such a strong wind.

Later the Coast Guard told us that they had recorded peak winds of 82 mph. I can't imagine being in a full hurricane with winds over 100 knots. I could hardly believe that our anchors hadn't dragged.

Jim: A few days later, in Beaufort, South Carolina, we met a French-Canadian sailor from Montreal who had encountered similar problems anchoring. I wish that I could remember his name or the name of his boat, because he saved us from untold future problems. Like us, he sailed a fin keeled* boat. The secret to anchoring a fin keeled boat in tidal waters, he told us, was to always use a sentinel anchor. Now I had read the articles on sentinel anchors (all of them I thought), but I had neither read nor heard of a sentinel put to that use. Nor have I since. But we tried it, and it worked. A fifteen pound mushroom anchor attached to the anchor line with a heavy brass shackle and lowered to a depth of anywhere from six feet to what we calculated to be just off the bottom at low tide worked to keep the rode* from floating up and getting caught behind the keel. In heavy wind conditions, we added another ten pound mushroom to it. The sailor who taught us the trick said he never used more than one anchor, but at times we found it convenient to use two to limit the scope of our swing. When we did, I just lashed the two rodes together about eight to twelve feet from the bow and ran the sentinel down the double rode. This seems like such a simple trick that I couldn't believe I'd never seen it in print.

After that we never hung up on our anchor line again. Angie, a strong convert to the idea that your best insurance on a boat is good ground tackle, bought herself a special present at the next opportunity, a thirty-three pound state of the art Bruce anchor. This, with thirty pounds of chain and a sentinel, held us through many a strong blow. The anchor was a wedding present to herself (another story) and now, more than thirty-five years later, sits in the garden outside our window.

Beaufort, S.C.

(Pronounced Bew-fort, unlike Beaufort, NC, named after the same man but pronounced Bow-fort.)

Angie: Beaufort, closest to the sea of all South Carolina cities, was one of our favorite stops along the waterway. Since many of our sailing friends were also anchored there, we decided to stay for the Thanksgiving holiday. Beaufort is a beautiful old city with many buildings that date to Antebellum and pre-Revolutionary days. The people also seemed to exhibit a friendliness and charm more common in earlier times. (In our stay in Beaufort nearly thirty years later, aboard *Bel Canto,* we learned a lot more about Beaufort's past during slavery times and its role during the Civil War.)

While we were in Beaufort we asked the waitress in a shorefront restaurant if there was a lumberyard. Jim wanted to buy a board to fix the dinghy seat, which had delaminated. She didn't think so, but then she said, " Maybe my husband Arthur can help you out." Arthur, who was rebuilding the three story Beaufort Inn from the inside out, took time to find a board and cut it to size for us. Then we chatted for a while, comparing life in the Midwest, where Arthur had toured as a golf pro, to life in Beaufort. Life in Beaufort seemed a lot more relaxed and peaceful.

Word got around that there was going to be a pig roast and pot-luck in Factory Creek on Thanksgiving night. Jackie, the dockmaster at the marina in Factory Creek, had been putting it on since 1957 and all boaters were welcome. I provided one of the highlights of the evening. When I went to step out of the dinghy onto the dock, dressed in my best clothes, I did the classic cartoon split. With one foot in the dinghy and the other on the dock, I felt them moving apart and I went straight down into the water. I was startled, but mostly angry because it seemed like everyone was watching me. I climbed back into the dinghy, sputtering and cursing like a true sailor. Jim took me back to *Escapade*, dried me off, and helped me wash out my clothes. I didn't need an introduction when I arrived at the marina the second time. One of the sailors joked that I was supposed to do that after the martinis, not before.

The potluck was probably the best we've ever been to. Jackie furnished the roast pig, roast goose, turkey, and alligator tail. The boaters had all knocked themselves out to outdo each other with the rest of the meal—breads, vegetables, salads, and at least fourteen kinds of dessert. It was a sumptuous feast. It was the first time that either of us had eaten roast pig or alligator tail. The alligator was bland and tough; it must have been an old gator. We much preferred the roast pig.

We sat in our shirt sleeves under the full moon, enjoying the feast and chatting with new and old friends, and wondered if life had any greater pleasures to offer.

Titusville, Florida

Dec. 16, 1985

Angie: After Jim proposed to me on the Niantic River, and I figured out it was a sincere proposal and accepted, we had decided to get married in the Bahamas. But when we reached Florida we got to thinking that, since we were both divorced, we might have to jump through hoops in the Bahamas and a Florida wedding might be wiser. Leona and Heinie, Jim's mother and stepfather, were planning to drive over to Titusville to meet us, but we didn't tell them or any of our boating friends of our plan. When we got to Titusville, we went to the courthouse to get a license and arrange for a civil ceremony to be performed by the county clerk. We had to get a blood test to prove that neither one of us had syphilis. That cost forty dollars and put a big hole in our twenty-five dollar a day budget. For wedding presents we bought Jim a fancy spear for spearfishing in the Bahamas, and I picked out a rigging knife and a thirty-three pound Bruce anchor. The Bruce anchor, the type used by oil rigs in the North Sea, was considered to be the best at the time and I figured we could use it after our experience in Charleston. More than thirty-five years later I still have the anchor *and* Jim.

Although we hadn't told any of our friends we were getting married, as we walked around Titusville that day I couldn't help exclaiming to everyone we crossed paths with, "I'm getting married tomorrow!" Jim laughed and said it reminded him of the song "Get Me to the Church On Time" in *My Fair Lady*. We just asked Heinie and Leona if they could meet us 9:30 the next morning because we had some errands to do. Once we were in the car with them we told them we were getting married at 11:00 and we wanted them to be our witnesses. They told us how happy they were for us, and I guess they were because Jim's mother had tears of happiness running down her cheeks. It was about forty-five minutes before the wedding when we got to a florist shop that I had spotted earlier. I dashed in and picked out some flowers for the florist to make bouquets for Jim's mom and me. The two bouquets cost all of eleven dollars. Jim claimed, I think facetiously, that the cost of the wedding, counting the blood tests, the fees for the license and the county clerk, and taking Leona and Heinie out to lunch afterwards was going to put us so far in the hole that we'd never be able to crawl out of it. "You only go around once," I told him. "We're not going to make it half way!" he replied. Anyway, the whole affair cost us about a hundred and twenty-five dollars.

When we got to the courthouse, the clerk asked us if we wanted to be married outside. Of course it was a lot more pleasant out on the grass under the trees than in a dingy courthouse office. The wedding party consisted of us, Leona and Heinie, and a young German glider pilot who Heinie and Leona had met in the campground where they were staying. He had visited us the day before and heard Jim talking to his brother Chuck on the ham radio about our wedding plans, but he hadn't said anything to Jim's folks. He just showed up, and it was serendipitous for us because he took the one photograph that we have of our wedding. And I have to tell you how we were dressed for the occasion (I didn't have a wide selection of clothes on the boat). The bride wore a long-sleeved white gauze blouse that she had picked up at a garage sale and a skirt that she had reconstructed from a sun dress bought on Martha's Vineyard years earlier. In her ears she sported a pair of hand-crafted silver earrings with black onyx stones set in them that the groom had bought in Norfolk and kept as a Christmas present for her. The groom was attired in a light blue cashmere wool sweater that his mother had given him and white jeans. They both wore boat shoes. The actual ceremony took about five minutes and

I cried through the whole thing. I think that, even though it was a civil ceremony, the clerk took it straight from the Baptist handbook. Anyway, Jim promised to Love, Honor, and Cherish me, while I had to promise to Love, Honor, and Obey him. How well do you think I've kept that last promise?

Heinie and Leona bought us a wedding cake and a basket with cheese, ham, and sparkling cider. We took them to lunch at a restaurant near the marina and the manager gave us a free bottle of wine and a small cake with a candle on it to add to the celebration. When we were back aboard *Escapade*, Sarah from the boat *Spray came* by, and later Roly and Gina from *Oborea* dropped by as well. They were surprised when we invited them to join our wedding reception, since we had told them that we were getting married in the Bahamas. Jim put together a dinner of deli sandwiches with provolone, pastrami, salami, and steamed quahogs that someone at the campground had given Heinie. This was served with champagne, followed by wedding cake and herbal tea. We had a great time talking and laughing for about six hours. It was a great celebration and everyone was shocked that without any planning it had turned into a real wedding.

Our wedding on the courthouse lawn

Later, when we were heading out of the harbor for West Palm Beach, I threw my wedding bouquet to the manatees.

Stocking Up

Angie: We had been told that food was very expensive in the Bahamas. Many goods, including water, were imported by boat, pushing prices up. A head of iceberg lettuce cost $2.50, cabbage $3.00, and a liter of club soda $1.90. That was a lot of money in 1985. Even water had to be paid for at $.25 a gallon. So we decided to stock up as much as we could before we crossed over to the Bahamas. Of course you carry a lot of canned goods when you are cruising on a small boat. We didn't have refrigeration and freeze-dried food hadn't become a thing yet. Canned and dried food were to be our staples, along with (we hoped) fresh fish that we would would catch or buy along the way.

When I first met Jim and cruised with him on the Great Lakes, we didn't quite agree on provisioning. I've always been a bit of a food snob, so the first thing that had to go was the Taster's Choice instant coffee. I was used to grinding my own beans for coffee, but this wasn't going to work on *Escapade*, since we didn't have electricity, so we compromised on high quality cans of ground coffee. The next thing to go was the canned corned beef. The noted round the world sailor Tristan Jones had this recipe for stew with corned beef hash. First you set the carrots, potatoes and onions to cooking. Then you open the cans of corned beef and throw half away because it's fat. Then you throw the other half away and eat the stewed vegetables. On our first trip, Jim also carried canned chicken. Now you might be thinking something similar to canned tuna or salmon, but this chicken was in a can the size of a tomato juice can. When Jim opened it and pulled out the carcass of a scrawny dead chicken, I took one look and said "No way! I would have to be starving to eat that!"

Since Jim's mother and stepfather had driven over to Titusville to meet us, we took advantage of their car to provision our boat, buying cases of canned goods at "Save-a-Lot" and rice and beans in bulk at the local health food store. (The rice turned out to be only "semi-vegetarian," i.e., loaded with hatching insects, and we had to dump it.) The list of food and cooking supplies that we carried was over three typed pages long, and every available space was stuffed. Among the essentials, in addition to different kinds of rice and beans, were flour, baking soda, pizza mix, sugar, maple syrup, dried Romano and Parmesan cheeses, peanut butter and jam, tomato paste, tomato sauce, and canned tomatoes (for pasta sauce), several kinds of dried pasta, canned potatoes and German potato salad, canned mushrooms, cream of celery soup used for several recipes, New England clam chowder but also canned clams and shrimp, canned tuna fish and salmon, canned chunk chicken, canned pineapple and grapefruit juice which would turn out to be just the thing for mixing with rum for the afternoon happy hour—well the list goes on and on, but you get the idea. In all we spent over fifteen hundred dollars in Titusville. Of course, that included the Bruce anchor that I bought for myself as a wedding present.

Chapter Ten:

Across the Gulf Stream to the Bahamas

Jim: The Gulf Stream has a terrible reputation among people who aren't familiar with it. A river that runs through the ocean, it is compressed as it makes its way northward between the Bahamas and Florida. A strong north wind against the current can kick up some wicked and dangerous seas, so you have to pick your time for a crossing. This area is part of the infamous "Bermuda Triangle," where many boats have been "mysteriously" lost. *Charlie's Crab* was one such boat. The boat, with the owner and his three guests aboard, was lost without a trace crossing from Cat Island to Fort Lauderdale. As I heard it, the skipper knew that a storm was predicted. An experienced sailor, he gambled that he could beat the storm in time to attend a party in Fort Lauderdale. He lost the gamble. There was nothing mysterious about that.

We sat in Lake Worth for a week waiting a break in the weather in order to cross. We'd welcomed the strong north wind that had brought us here from Titusville, but it was kicking up seas too heavy for us to risk crossing in our light-weight boat designed for Great Lakes sailing. But on the day before Christmas Eve the wind calmed and the prediction was for at least twenty four hours of favorable weather.

Common practice was to make the crossing at night so that you could approach West End in morning light. We would be sailing from water half a mile deep to where the deepest channels would be eight feet deep sprinkled with coral reefs that could wreck your boat if you didn't see them.

Angie: Jim was more worried about the seas on the Gulf Stream and I was worried about the reefs once we got to the other side. We listened to the NOAA weather forecast which was for calm seas and decided this was the time to go. At five in the afternoon we were still feeling the effects of the cold front that had brought us here, and we were dressed in several layers, starting with long underwear on the bottom and foul weather gear on top.

There was still light when we hauled anchor and began making our way down the last few miles of the waterway and through Palm Beach Harbor. We hoped to have enough light take us all the way out to the ocean, but in the event, the darkness caught us and we had to pilot out in the dark anyway. The night was mostly overcast, with occasional drizzle, but often the nearly full moon broke through the clouds, and even when we couldn't see the moon, it was light enough to see the horizon. It was also getting progressively warmer. We gradually shed layers of clothes, and by the time we reached West End, at about 9. a.m., we were in T-shirts.

Jim set our course for well south of our destination, West End, because we knew that the current would carry us to the north. The water in the Gulf Stream is warmer than the surrounding water, which is one way you know when you have entered it. The wind was light so we used our engine to assist keeping us at a comfortable four or five knots, and the water was remarkably smooth. Of course we were tethered to life lines that ran from the bow to the stern of the boat, as we always were when sailing at night or in strong weather. We steered a course of 125 (SE) to make good a course of 098 magnetic. At times the LORAN showed us going 065 (NE) and at times 112 (SE), at a speed varying from 2.8 to 12 knots. That's how the Gulf Stream affected us.

By six o'clock we spotted the lights of West End almost directly ahead and by seven we were opposite the settlement. Jim said we should wait a little longer before trying to enter the channel, which was only marked by a single light, till the sun was high enough to read the water. At first, we couldn't make out where the entrance to the harbor was, but then we watched a commercial boat, the *Jack Tar*, go in and a sailboat come out. Suddenly the configuration fell into place. The depth of the water goes very quickly from a half mile to a few feet. It was beautiful and scary when we could suddenly see the bottom through the clear blue water. It looked like we were barely clearing the bottom when our depth sounder was still reading thirty feet. I was able to see the reefs on either side as we entered the channel. This was a skill I was going to become very proficient at before we left the Bahamas. We made it through safely, but we did see one boat that had tried for the channel earlier and got hung up on a reef. He sat there rocking gently and waiting for the tide, which fortunately was rising. And even more fortunately, he wasn't taking on water and sinking!

By eight thirty we were tied to the marina dock at West End. We couldn't leave the boat until we had cleared customs, but that didn't bother us, as we were both ready to crash. At about eleven we heard knock on the boat. We looked out and saw a tall, elegantly dressed black man sporting a gold Rolex watch. We invited him aboard and he sat at the dinette while we filled out immigration forms and answered questions. When we had finished and he got up to leave, he looked back at poster of Hope Carlton and, grinning, commented, "Nice picture!"

Grand Bahamas to the Abacos

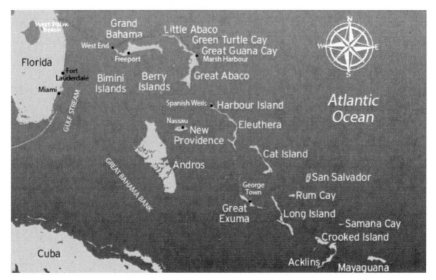

Our route from West Palm Beach to Georgetown, Exuma

As soon as we were in the marina at West End, we began making new friends. People who live aboard their sailboats form a community, and because of the transient nature of the sailing life, newcomers are accepted immediately and friendships formed quickly. At least that's the way we found it on this trip thirty some years ago. John and Sue, from Whirlygig, moored next to us, filled us in on where to shop and what was going on in the village. Their son Brian, who was eight years old and sharp as a tack, had spent half his life on a boat. We thought what a great education he was getting.

Jim: On Christmas Eve day—in the afternoon after we arrived—I walked into the village about a mile and a half away, to see what I could scrape up for Christmas dinner. The village was poor and plain, like some of the remote villages I'd seen in Spain and Greece, with not a tourist place anywhere. The few tourists stuck to the hotel down near the marina. There were three liquor stores (called wholesale liquor outlets) and two tiny, old fashioned grocery stores. There were also some administrative offices in what looked like an old warehouse. The only modern looking building was the yellow brick police station. I was able to buy a frozen chicken for $3.75, and for Christmas dinner we had southern fried chicken, wine, dressing, gravy, and cranberry sauce. It was delicious!

On the day after Christmas I wrote this in my journal: "5:00 a.m. The wind is howling and swooning through the masts of a 92 foot sailboat moored in the nearby commercial harbor, and the surf pounds the bank with a steady roar. Even here in the well protected harbor stray gusts of wind catch us and *Escapade* strains at the mooring lines. I'm glad to be here and not anchored out in the bank someplace, even though it's costing us $20 a day."

The Bahamians celebrate Christmas all night long, ending with a communal breakfast from 4 to 8 a. m. followed by the Junkanoo, a traditional Bahamian Boxing Day costume parade. Jim and Marty, from *Snapdragon*, a couple we had met in St. Augustine, invited us to see the festivities with them. Jim was a retired assistant school superintendent, and Marty, who was about thirty years younger, was a free-lance court reporter. Our path kept intersecting with people we had met along the waterway, and we were always glad to see each other. This is what I mean by the community of cruising sailors.

Angie: We got up at 5:30 to catch the parade and have breakfast. The village is about two miles from the marina, and we got there too late for the parade. But even though we missed the parade, we did have a real Bahamian breakfast of fish stew, grouper cooked in beef broth, served with Johnnycake bread.

The weather was still windy and cold from the front that was moving through. I was tired from the four mile hike into the village and back, and besides, 5:30 is way too early for me to get up in the morning (unless we are going to sail). I took advantage of being in civilization to do the laundry. This took me a couple of hours because there were only two washers and one dryer, and it seemed like all of the people from the hotel had come down to do their laundry at the same time. I couldn't believe it!

By the Friday after Christmas the front had passed and we had a beautiful day. We left West End at about nine, sailed about eight miles up past Sandy Cay, and then reentered the Little Bahama Bank. Once again we had the experience of going from depths that wouldn't read on the depth sounder to under eight feet of water.

Jim: Before we left Ann Arbor I threw away my old fishing pole, which had a broken tip. I planned to buy another one on the way to the Bahamas, but that was one of the things that didn't get done. Now I regretted it, as I wanted to try trolling from the boat. I was lamenting not having a rod when Angie said, "Stop complaining. Be like Tristan Jones. Rig something up." ("Be like Tristan Jones" became one of her favorite sayings. If you've read any of this indomitable sailor's books, you'll understand.) So I improvised a pole out of a spare man overboard pole tip and a clevis ring, clamped my reel to the stern pulpit, and rigged up a line. I had only 6 pound test line, which wasn't the best for trolling. Anyway, just as we were entering the bank I got a strike and reeled in a small yellowtail snapper. After that I lost two lures and all my line, either on strikes or weeds, and that ended my fishing for the time being.

Later on I was able to get some 50 pound test line and rigged it to a mop handle stuck in the flag holder with a clothes pin so that it would pop off and, I hoped, set the hook when the momentum of the boat took up the slack. I never did have much luck fishing, though. Aside from one small grouper, we caught several barracuda, which we were afraid to eat because some of them are toxic from the coral reefs where they feed. And several times we had dorado (mahi mahi) on the line, and they made a beautiful sight as they changed colors when they danced on the waves at the end of the line. But they had soft mouths and we never succeeded in getting one to the boat. The most spectacular catch we had was a wahoo that came straight up out of the water after it was hooked, but it too got free before we could get it in. With a proper fishing pole we might have done better. When we bought *Bel Canto,* we inherited two fine deep sea fishing rods, but we never did get a chance to use them. Anyway, Angie took the yellowtail and made a delicious Bahamian fish stew in the pressure cooker with potatoes, carrots and onions and seasoned with a little spicy Old Bay seasoning.

Angie: (Saturday, December 28) Our first anchorage in the Bahamas was Mangrove Cay, about thirty miles from West End. The water was beautiful! It was really weird to be able to see the bottom gliding under the boat. I was learning to know the depth by reading the color of the water. While doing this I had to keep an eye out for the dark patches that marked coral reefs. This became second nature after a while. There were few navigational aids, unlike in the states with numerous buoys and ranges. In the Bahamas you have to read your charts carefully and pay close attention to the color of the water and to your depth sounder. It was exciting and a little scary at the same time. It felt so good to be under sail again. We had scarcely sailed between entering the waterway at Norfolk at Mile One and leaving it at West Palm Beach at mile 1018. Now, finally, we were a sailboat again.

The anchorages on the Grand Bahamas banks are nothing like we were used to on the Great Lakes, where there are well protected coves and harbors everywhere you go. Here you tucked in on the lee side of a cay and hoped that the wind direction stayed the same through the night. The prevailing wind was pretty dependably from the east, unless a front was moving through, so this usually worked out pretty well. There was a lot of rolling and pitching on the night that we spent at Mangrove Cay. I made a fish stew with the yellowtail Jim had caught, which we ate with homemade cornbread. I also made a pound cake in the pressure cooker. It was all gone in less than a day.

Jim: From Mangrove Cay we went on to Great Sale Cay, our last stop before the Abacos. The Abacos are to the East of Grand Bahama Island, so we motored into an east wind most of the way there. We anchored on the lee side of the island, and I put on my wetsuit hoping to get us some spiny lobsters for dinner, but the tide was out and I couldn't get in around the edges where the lobsters hang out. I never did have any luck getting lobsters, or spearing fish with the new spear Angie had bought me, for that matter. Later, in the Abacos and the Exumas, I did manage to get plenty of conch. These large snail like creatures crawled along the bottom and couldn't outswim me or duck into hiding places to escape me.

Angie: We ate a lot of conch when we were in the Bahamas. Before you eat conch, you have to pound the heck out of it, because it's a muscle and very tough. Somewhere along the way we acquired an old hand cranked meat grinder that we used to grind up the conch and make great conch burgers. But first Jim had to get the conch out of its shell. This involved whacking the shell in a certain place with a hammer to free the muscle and then pulling it out of the shell. It was usually dusk (sundown always came at six o'clock) when Jim got around to doing this. Since he had to do it out on the deck, it became a battle with the mosquitoes. As Jim said, we didn't have much luck fishing, but fortunately you could always buy fresh or freshly frozen fish from the local fishermen, so we had plenty of great fish dinners.

Jim: During the night at Great Sale Cay the wind switched to the southwest, blowing right into the open side of the cay. The change in the motion of the boat woke me and I got up at 12:30, hooked up our new 33 pound Bruce anchor to its thirty feet of chain, loaded it all in the dinghy, and rowed it out to windward to set a second anchor. After that Angie and I stayed up about an hour and a half playing cribbage to make sure that we were going to hold (I won three dollars), and finally went back to sleep. In the morning we hated to get up, but we knew that we had to get an early start—at least by seven—to reach Green Turtle Cay in one day. There was no safe place to stop with the southwest wind blowing. We were up at 6:30, washed our hair, and were underway with the dawn at seven. Once out of the anchorage, we raised our sails and had a glorious sail all day long, averaging six knots most of the day. For five hours we had the spinnaker up. The wind was about 12 knots, the sky blue, the temperature about 70 degrees—an idyllic day! We arrived at Green Turtle Cay on a dying wind, just at dusk. We sailed into the anchorage on a rising tide (we couldn't have made it through the entrance channel at low tide), dropped the Bruce over the bow, swung in behind two other boats, and dropped the main. Just as we finished, darkness set in.

Green Turtle Cay

Jim: The Abaco Island group in the Bahamas is a sailor's paradise. We had chartered a boat there a year earlier to familiarize ourselves with the area. It was the kind of place people dream of when they think of sailing in tropical islands—steady breezes, beautiful palm studded anchorages, clear blue water, and quaint villages. And the whole area is protected from heavy winds and seas. It seemed to us like someone had designed a playground for sailors. If your only sailing experience was here, you'd have a very unrealistic and idealized picture of what the sailing life is like. It's no wonder that many permanent live-aboards, like our friends Jack and Donna on *Horizon*, ended up staying here.

New Plymouth, on Green Turtle Cay, was our introduction to what it was like to live in Paradise. It, like the the whole of the Abacos, was settled by Loyalists after the American Revolution. Later former Africans who had escaped either from slave ships or from the forced labor camps (i.e., plantations) in the United States became the dominant segment of the population. New Plymouth is a neat, crowded little town, with everything in miniature. The streets are just wide enough for a small European car to get down. I think there were only about a dozen cars in town. Most of the residents either walked or rode around in electric golf carts. On our first day we walked the narrow streets, ate a lunch of conch fritters, a conch burger and cole slaw at the Sea View Restaurant, bought a loaf of fresh baked bread and a half dozen eggs for $3.50 at one of the two local grocery stores, bought six lobster tails for our dinner from a local fisherman for $6.50, and then returned to *Escapade*.

Green Turtle Cay is a picture book perfect "Tropical Island," with colorful houses tucked in under waving palm trees, surrounded by water ranging from gold to turquoise to deep blue. The Bahamians themselves were a bit stand-offish. I didn't blame them. They were inundated with tourists who didn't show much inclination to understand them. The exceptions were the young men who made their living diving for crawfish (spiny lobsters) and conch and who held quite an attraction for the young women (and not so young) off the boats.

These same men were the center of attention on New Years Eve, at the dance up at the Rooster View, perched on the highest hill in Green Turtle Cay, maybe 200 feet above sea level. We danced to the music of the Gully Roosters, a local group that played a wide variety of music to a reggae beat. One of the Bahamians, tall, good looking, dressed in a colorful island shirt, was a particularly good dancer, and all of the women from the boats, including Angie, were eager to dance with him. I can't remember if I felt a twinge of jealousy, but Angie still loves to dance, and I love to watch her almost as much as to dance with her.

On New Year's Day we finally got to witness the Junkanoo parade that we had missed in West End. Men and women in colorful costumes made of strips of paper—yellow and black or pink and black—marched and danced down the street to the music of drums made of hides stretched over steel barrels, cow bells, and whistles. At each end of the main street they stopped to tighten their drumheads over fires made of scrap paper and cardboard. This took me back to when I played drums in the high school band in the mid fifties. Our drumheads back then were also made of hides (now they are plastic) and the tone of the snare drums would get lower and lower as we marched. Marching in the rain was always a disaster, since the drumheads would get soggy and drumsticks would go right through them. We could have used something to warm them, and our hands as well! The parade started at three in the afternoon, and the music continued until well after dark. We had no trouble hearing it in the anchorage.

Banished from Paradise

The easiest way to get to the village from the anchorage was to use the dinghy landing at a marina called The Other Side Club. As we were coming back to the boat from one trip to town Angie reached up and picked a lemon hanging from a tree next to the path. (I'd given her the idea by picking one earlier, up on the edge of town.) It seemed like a natural thing to do in this island paradise. But the owner of the marina witnessed the act and came after us very angry. He gave us a stern lecture that ended with the line, "I wasn't born hard; it's people who make me hard." Then he told us he didn't want to see us using his landing again. I was ashamed because people in the Abacos really do respect each other's property. Theft was rare. Taking a lemon didn't seem like a big deal, but if all the people cutting through his lot picked one, his trees would be stripped. We hadn't thought about the lemons actually belonging to someone, but there it was.

Fortunately there was another dinghy landing. The path to town went right through a private yard, but the owners, who have an outboard shop, didn't seem to mind. They even turned on a light on New Year's Eve to help us find our way back to the boat. The path through the woods was badly rutted and with thick roots and could be perilous in the dark. On New Year's Day we stayed in town longer than we expected, having a drink and jawing with other sailors at the Blue Bee Bar. When we left it was pitch dark and we had to feel our way down the path. We couldn't see a thing and hung on to each other like a couple of kids. If we hadn't been down that path before we would have gotten hopelessly lost.

Green Turtle Cay was one of our favorite places to visit as long as we were in the Abacos, but we never did go back to The Other Side Club.

———～———

We hung out in the Abacos for a couple of months, and it was a perfect place to entertain visitors. Mike Sepanski, who originally was supposed to be my sailing partner when I first started thinking about this cruise, came down for a two week visit. Fortunately, he didn't hold a grudge because of the fact that I had replaced him with Angie as my crew. And my daughter Kari, a nursing student at Eastern Michigan University, spent her winter break with us. We had a great time exploring, getting to know the area, and meeting lots of folks who were semi-permanent members of the cruising fraternity. Kari got to experience conch burgers and tuna sandwiches made with real tuna.

Life in the Abacos was not total paradise for me, though. For one thing, there were boat problems to deal with. The two horse Evinrude on our dinghy kept conking out. Even though I'd taken a small engine repair course in Ann Arbor in preparation for this adventure, my periodic efforts at taking the carburetor apart and cleaning it, replacing the spark plug, and performing other maintenance tasks didn't provide a permanent solution. Besides, our new cruising friends advised us that if we were to get to the best fishing spots, we would need a better dinghy and at least a nine horsepower motor. I proved this when I took Mike out to a reef to do some snorkeling and nearly killed us both. As we approached the reef we could see the waves coming in on the ocean side and occasionally breaking over the reef, even though there was very little wind. I told Mike to be ready with the viewing bucket (a bucket with a glass bottom which gives you a clear view through the surface of the water) while I maneuvered the dinghy up on the leeward side of the reef. Although we were getting bounced around a bit, I didn't think I'd have much trouble holding the dinghy in place for Mike. But then, as he had his head down looking through the bucket, I saw a big wave coming. It was a curler, and it came over the reef and caught the dinghy, sending it up in the air. For a moment I thought we could stay in the dinghy, but then we found ourselves and all of our gear in the water. The dinghy miraculously stayed right side up, and with the motor still running it was making small circles. We managed to get ourselves into the dinghy and started collecting our gear, the net bag with our snorkeling gear in it, Mike's pack, paddles, the dinghy seat and the 35mm camera that Mike had borrowed from a friend. Fortunately he had wrapped it in two ziplock bags and the camera stayed dry, even though everything else we had was soaked. The only thing we didn't retrieve was the viewing bucket, which turned out to be irreplaceable. As we rounded the edge of the cay heading back for the harbor at Man-of-War, the motor died and wouldn't restart. We were now in calm water, but it was still a long row back.

A Fish Story

Angie had bought me a good sling spear in Florida and we looked forward to eating our fill of fresh fish, lobsters, and conch while in the Bahamas. These entries from my journal tell how that worked out.

"Twice we've made it around to the other side of the island, where the fishing and lobstering is supposed to be good. The first time it was too windy to swim. The surf was crashing in and the tide was going out, bouncing us around perilously in our rubber dinghy, so we turned around and came back. But yesterday was calm and we went out again. On the ocean side of Green Turtle Cay there is a large bay protected by reefs and islands. We went swimming and found a couple of holes full of colorful fish. I picked up one conch and saw a couple of large fish from the boat, but nothing I could get close enough to spear. Later, on our way to the dinghy dock, Dave, who lives here year around on his Cal 25, waved us over. He had one more hog snapper filet than he could use and offered it to us for dinner. His partner said, 'We also got three lobsters, but we had to eat those.' They told us that the good fishing was by a reef just beyond the one we had been going to." The snapper, served with left over bean soup over rice, made one of the best fish dinners I have ever eaten and whetted our appetite to do more fishing!

My next journal entry says: "We've made four trips to the reef, and so far I haven't caught anything for us by myself. It's a good hour's trip out there, around the end of Green Turtle and past No Name Cay, put-putting in our rubber dinghy with the two horsepower motor. The day after we talked to Dave, the weather was calm and Angie and I dinghied out to the reef he had described. I saw lots of fish, including a barracuda about four feet long, which swam up and stared me in the face. I also saw a huge shark as we were approaching the reef and another in the water. That was the end of that day's fishing for me. Dave later told me that the sharks we saw near the bottom were nurse sharks and that they wouldn't bother us. It's the ones that approach near the surface that you have to watch out for. He also told us that the barracuda wouldn't bother us as long as we weren't wearing anything shiny.

"Later we met Carroll Sawyer, a local fisherman. He worked for the airlines for 15 years and has traveled to Wisconsin, Chicago, Ireland, and so on. Now he's back diving for lobsters. The locals are allowed to dive with compressors and they get tons. He told us the reef is better over by Manjack Cay. Someday we'll take *Escapade* over and try our luck there.

"Saturday we went back to No Name Cay. Dave was already there and gave me a lesson in where and how to fish. He uses weights, dives right into the coral, which grows like great trees under the water, and hangs on with one hand while he goes after the lobsters with his spear. He gave us the two lobsters he got while demonstrating. I tried for a while. It was rougher and colder than Friday. Angie sat in the boat, which was occasionally tossed around by the surf breaking over the reef. With my wetsuit on, but no weights, I was too buoyant to go after lobster. I saw a couple of grouper, but they kept their distance and I didn't get a shot at them. One led me into some shallow coral where

I was afraid of getting caught in the surf and cut to ribbons. Angie noticed the sky turning black in the southwest and we decided to head for home. We made it back to *Escapade* just ahead of the rain."

Later on I bought weights and was able to free dive to depths of twenty feet or more holding my breath—enough to gather all of the conch we could eat. But I never did master the art of spear fishing. Luckily for us we ate plenty of fresh fish due to the generosity of other more adept sailors and the ready availability from local fishermen. Nevertheless, seeing the schools of colorful fish—brightly colored parrot fish mixed in with the bright blues and yellows of other species—made our trips to the reefs a great experience. [Angie: I was pretty impressed with Jim's ability to free dive twenty feet holding his breath. Later on, when I started swimming laps in the pool I realized how challenging this was.]

More about Food

Angie: Since we didn't have refrigeration, fresh vegetables and leftovers were a problem. Cabbage kept better than lettuce, so we ate more cole slaw than salads. We learned that if you peeled the leaves off the head of cabbage (or lettuce, for that matter), rather than cutting it, it lasted longer. For salads, we ate tomatoes, carrots, peppers and onions without the lettuce. We'd keep leftover fish and meat dishes for a day and then heat them up well in the pressure cooker. We never had a problem. We found that mayonnaise keeps perfectly well without refrigeration as long as you don't contaminate it with utensils that have already handled food. I still practice that.

We had beer in the hold when we left Florida for the Bahamas, but since the water temperature was around 80 degrees, we soon grew tired of warm beer. Bartenders always looked puzzled when we'd go to a bar or restaurant and I'd ask for a COLD beer. Their beer was alway served ice cold, and they didn't know where I was coming from. Happy hours are big among boaters, and we found that rum and pineapple juice, even unchilled, went better than warm Heinekens.

The island women were another great source of food in the islands. On Sundays they would offer roast chicken, black eyed peas, potato salad, and home made bread for sale to the boaters, and that was always a delicious feast. In Marsh Harbour, the locals usually threw a steak barbecue on Saturday and Sunday nights, serving New York strip steaks cooked to your specifications along with baked potatoes and salad. Not a bad meal if you didn't mind an occasional rat running over your feet.

Of course we did a lot of cooking aboard, since we were on a strict budget. Jim made risotto with arborio rice, chicken and sausage, using curry rather than saffron for seasoning. Even though I am Italian, this was the first time I'd eaten risotto. I made fish stew and faux chicken soup using canned chicken and bouillon cubes for stock. In fact, we invented all kinds of recipes depending on what we had on board.

Green Turtle Cay-A Squall

Jim: As I mentioned earlier, when we first arrived at Black Sound Harbour, in Green Turtle Cay, we sailed in and dropped our anchor, the Bruce that Angie had bought herself for a wedding present in Titusville, Florida. We felt pretty smug about our seamanship. Etiquette in the Bahamas called for putting out two anchors opposite each other so that you would swing in a smaller circle, making room for more boats to anchor, so I also set the CQR (also called a plow because of its shape). In the first norther that came along we dragged the Bruce about 75 yards before it caught again. The plow just slid across the bottom. Luckily there were few boats in the anchorage and we dragged straight up the sound without colliding with anything. I reset the Bruce and the plow and we sat in the middle of the sound for a couple of days.

One morning, about nine, we decided to go to Man-of-War Cay where our friends Jack and Donna hung out in *Horizon*, their beautiful 39 foot Alden ketch. We wanted to get down there before the next cold front came through. The trip from Green Turtle to Man-of-War requires good weather because you have to go out into the Atlantic through Whale Cay Passage, which is notorious for wild surf breaking across the bar. These sea conditions are called rages and several boats have been lost in them. By the time we got our anchors up and were ready to go we found that the tide had gone down too far for us to leave the sound. The entrance has only about four feet at low water, and we needed five to get through.

We tried to reanchor near our old spot, but the Bruce wouldn't catch. I went on down the sound looking for a spot clear of weeds on the bottom. Finally I found a spot that looked promising, so we dropped the Bruce and backed down on it as hard as we could. After it was set, I went swimming with the snorkel and saw that it was completely buried. I also noticed some large sections of the bottom, at least six feet in diameter and sixteen inches thick, that were standing up on edge, as though they had been peeled off the bottom. Later I figured that that's just what had happened. Since we had plenty of room to swing, I didn't put down another anchor, but I did run the mushroom anchor down the rode as a sentinel to keep the anchor line from fouling on the keel. We'd learned that lesson the hard way.

Around eight in the evening Angie had risotto cooking on the stove, made with rice and leftover chicken soup, and I was attempting to play the guitar a little, when a squall line hit. We watched great sheets of water being blown almost horizontally by thirty to forty knot winds. (Later we had over three inches of water in the dinghy.)

For a while it looked like we were going to hold. I was worried that the couple of boats anchored upwind of us would drag into us. Then suddenly I felt the bow swing and saw the light on a dock on shore bearing down on us. We were moving fast, right into the shallow water. I jumped into the cockpit and started the engine. Throwing it into forward gear, I started to bring the bow up into the wind when the motor died. I'd forgotten to push the choke back in. I restarted and got moving again. I could see the dock about ten yards from the boat, and I prayed that there would be deep water up to it, but I knew that the water shallowed up near shore. I peered nearsightedly at the depth sounder (my glasses were useless in that downpour) and saw that it read MSD (for missed). It reads that when the bottom is more than 200 feet down—or when we were aground! I had the tiller hard over to starboard, but for a moment I felt the bow drift to starboard and I was sure that we were aground. Then *Escapade* turned and came up into the wind. We may actually have been aground, but the bottom was so soft that we plowed our own channel out.

By this time Angie was up on deck in her foul weather gear. I sent her forward with a light to see where the anchor line was. I was afraid of fouling it on the prop. That would have been disastrous. Fortunately, the sentinel was keeping it down. I just motored slowly into the wind until the worst of the squall was over. The wind shifted from the northwest to the northeast and was blowing us away from the shore that we had been on, but there was still another shore and anchored boats to leeward of us. I made one attempt at resetting the Bruce, but it wouldn't hold. Angie spotted a mooring buoy and suggested that we grab it, so I hauled up the anchor as she held the boat steady, and we headed for the buoy. It took us three passes to get it. [Angie: As that was happening, I knew that I couldn't fail.] On the last pass, Angie held onto the buoy with the boat hook for dear life as the bow of the boat swung across it. The boat hook collapsed, but Angie held on and we finally were secure. I figured that there was another large patch of bottom upended in the sound.

After all the excitement, we went down and polished off the risotto, which was still warm. Angie says that I can always eat, no matter what's going on. This time, she ate pretty well, too.

After the Squall *(from Jim's journal)*

"Today I did some washing in the rainwater we'd collected in the dinghy after the squall. Water costs fifteen cents a gallon, and we've been carrying it to the boat in five-gallon jugs, so we take advantage of every bit of free water we can get. When I was done with the washing, I unpacked my guitar, repaired a broken string, and practiced for a while. It's been eight months since I've played, so I'm laboriously trying to relearn all the music that I used to know by heart. It's difficult. My fingers are stiff and awkward, and my memory shot to hell—to say nothing of my fingernails.

"Don, of *Deja Vu*, the weatherman, was right. We're getting one norther after another. When the wind comes through, it blows thirty knots or better. It is definitely too cold and windy to go swimming and diving, so we stay on the boat reading and doing chores, napping in the afternoon to make up for the sleep we lose at night listening to the wind howl. We go into town to buy an item or two at the marine store or grocery store, or maybe to get a conch burger or hamburger at Seaview Restaurant. We're running out of good books to read. We're looking forward to getting to Man-of-War Cay where Jack and Donna, our good friends from Ann Arbor, are staying aboard *Horizon*. Jack had studied for a Ph. D. in literature and their boat is always well stocked with books."

More about Water

As I wrote in my journal, the front that came through was accompanied by torrential rains. Some friends told us that they had collected 100 gallons of water. That was quite a savings at 15 cents a gallon. I wasn't set up to collect water but I scooped about 10 gallons out of the dinghy. It looked and tasted okay, so I poured it into the auxiliary water bladder that we'd installed in Toronto. After that I figured out how to reverse the sail cover to make a trough that would collect water coming down the mast and drain into a bucket hung on the end of the boom. It became a standing joke that every time we had a storm, Angie would send me out on the deck to collect water, thunder and lightning be damned.

On to Man-of-War Cay

As soon as the weather settled we decided to head down to Man-of-War Cay. The wind had shifted to the west and was blowing ten to fifteen knots when we left. The offshore winds calmed the swells at Whale Cay Passage, hence there were no rages, and we sailed through under reefed main and partially furled genoa. I was still a little on edge because it was unfamiliar water and the hazards were serious. Whale Cay Passage takes you out into the ocean around a nearly impassable bar. We didn't see one patch of rocks until we were past them, but we were right on course and well clear of them. Once we were safely back in Abaco Sound we got some squalls. The wind picked up and *Escapade* flew down to Man-of-War Cay. When we approached the entrance between Sandy Cay and Man-of-War I wasn't sure we were in the right place. The chart showed fourteen to eighteen feet of water, but our depth sounder showed only eight. But we were in the right place.

The entrance to Man-of-War is a narrow, twisting passage through rock. Angie couldn't believe we were going to go through.

The wind was howling through the narrows, and we couldn't see the end of the channel. We crept under motor up to what looked like the entrance, with Angie at the bow. At the last minute, I turned away. The boat hardly moved against the wind and the current and I wondered if my transmission was going out. I waited for a motorboat to enter the channel and then we took another pass and went in. Later on we gathered enough confidence to enter this channel at night, and when our friends Roly and Ginny on the catamaran Oborea arrived, Angie boarded their boat to pilot them through the channel.

Angie: Ginnie was crying as we entered. When I went below I learned that Ginnie was scared to death of sailing. She had no sailing skills because Roly hadn't taught her any. After that experience I frequently lectured captains about teaching their partners some sailing skills.

In Man-of-War Cay we reconnected with Gordon and Donna from *Donna X*. Gordon was a Newfie and one of those people who seem capable of fixing anything. We had met Gordon in Beaufort, North Carolina, and I credited him with saving our relationship. Before setting off on our trip Jim had replaced the alcohol burners on the stove on *Escapade* with kerosene burners, thinking that kerosene would be more available in the Caribbean and also more efficient than alcohol. Alcohol is the safest and cleanest fuel, but it is slow. Anyway, we'd had nothing but trouble with our kerosene burners. They required frequent cleaning, and Jim had replaced them more than once. By the time we reached Beaufort, one wasn't working at all and the other only sporadically. We had just anchored in the harbor at Beaufort, N.C., when Gordon came rowing by in his dinghy and asked if there was anything we needed. "Do you know anything about kerosene stoves?" I asked him. "I have a Ph.D in kerosene stoves," Gordon replied. "Good," I said. "Maybe you can save our relationship. I'm about ready to jump ship." Gordon came aboard and soon there were parts of the burners spread all over the cockpit. As Gordon cleaned and reassembled them he threw piece after piece overboard, saying "You don't need this." When it was all together again he gave us some tips on maintaining it. So when Gordon saw us in Man-of-War his first question was "How's your stove and your love life?" We told him that both were fine.

Horizon

Our friends Jack and Donna Jacobs had a permanent mooring for *Horizon* in Man-Of-War Cay. Jim had helped them learn how to sail aboard *Escapade* back in the Great Lakes. Both of us had gone with them to pick their new boat *Horizon* up in Delaware and deliver it to the Chesapeake where they would start their journey via the Intracoastal Waterway to the Bahamas. Now they were fulfilling their dream of living in the islands. Jack had been a Ph.D. candidate in literature and their boat was a virtual library. As Donna said, where other people stored food, they had books. Of course, this was before you could carry an entire library on your iPad. We had a dozen or so books for general reading in addition to our navigation and sailing library, and we tried to trade with other sailors when we could. Most other sailors, though, seemed to have mostly books by people like Danielle Steele, or at best, Stephen King, and so it was real treat to be able to trade with or borrow books from someone who valued good writing the way we did. It was Jack who introduced us to Ann Patchett and the book *Bel Canto*. Ann Patchett became one of our favorite authors. Later, when we named our next boat *Bel Canto*, it would bring memories of the idyllic days we spent in the Abacos and dreams of similar adventures to come.

Chapter Eleven:

From the Abacos to the Exumas

Jim: As I've said, the Abacos were a sailor's paradise—beautiful anchorages, protected waters, and plenty of opportunities to socialize with other sailors and to get immersed in island life. As we write this, the Abacos and much of Grand Bahama Island have been devastated by Hurricane Dorian. A category five storm with wind gusts up to 220 miles an hour, it decided to squat on the islands for a full day and a half. We wonder how long it will be, if ever, for life in the islands to get back to anything resembling normal. In the midst of the COVID-19 pandemic, we wonder the same thing for ourselves.

We lingered in the Abacos for two months, enjoying solitary anchorages and island life in Green Turtle Cay, Hopetown and Marsh Harbor, where we indulged ourselves in the local food and drink: Methuselah Rum and Goombay Smashes, roast chicken dinners with homemade potato salad or rice and peas prepared by the island ladies for sale to the sailors, conch burgers, and ceviche, fresh fish and spiny lobsters. And where we spent our evenings dancing to or just lying out at night and listening to the island music.

When we finally decided it was time to leave the Abacos, we worked our way down to Little Harbor, at the south end of Abaco Sound and close to the outlet to the ocean where we would begin our passage to the Eleuthera and the Exumas. The entrance to Little Harbor carries only six feet at high tide, and we arrived at low tide, so we spent a very uncomfortable night anchored in the bight of Old Robinson, exposed to the sound of the surf breaking on the reefs and the swells from the ocean. In the morning at high tide we entered the harbor and took a mooring vacated by one of the boats that was taking advantage of the high tide to leave. Little Harbor was a popular place for sailors to visit, and had become one of our favorites, mainly because of the settlement established by the sculptor Randolph Johnston. Johnston, 82 years old and still very active when we were there, had sailed into the harbor when he was in his forties and decided that that was where he wanted to live and raise his family. He, his wife, and their two small children spent a few nights in a bat filled cave while he established a camp. When Angie and I explored the same cave, she was totally freaked out thinking that the bats would get tangled in her hair. By the time we visited Little Harbor, Johnston had a comfortable home with a workshop where he forged his sculptures that were sold worldwide. His sons had a cabana where they sold drinks to the visiting sailors.

Tale of the (not so ancient) mariner

While in Little Harbor we met Richard and Christine, a young French couple, at a cocktail party aboard *Carranda*, a 56 foot ketch. Richard and Christine had built their 30 foot sailboat *Christine* in Florida, using parts and materials that they had scavenged for or bought cheaply. They were planning to sail it across the Atlantic back home to France. We were full of curiosity about anyone who had done or who planned to do a trans ocean passage, and Angie and Richard were soon engaged in conversation. This is a condensed version of Richard's story.

"We were anchored overnight about 20 miles east of Bimini on our way to New Providence when Hurricane Bob crossed Florida from the Gulf of Mexico and headed up the East Coast. We weren't in the path of the storm, but the winds picked up to 40 knots or more. I had set two anchors, and though *Christine* was bouncing around a bit, I felt she was secure. It was early morning when I felt one of the anchor lines go. I put on my bathing suit and mask and went over the side to check the shackle on the other line."

As Richard got down to the anchor, that line parted too, and the boat started drifting downwind with Christine aboard. She threw the man overboard pole* with life preserver and strobe light attached toward him, but soon lost sight of him in the rough seas and heavy rain. The wind carried the boat farther away. She struggled to start the outboard motor, but couldn't get it going. By the time she had raised the mainsail and got the boat under control, there was no sign of Richard or the man overboard flag.

Richard continued, "As the boat and Christine disappeared from view I could just make out the lights on Bimini and decided to try to swim for that island. After dawn I couldn't see the lights anymore and had trouble knowing what direction to swim in. I knew if I missed Bimini I would be swept into the Gulf Stream and that would be the end for me. The wind and currents kept sweeping me in different directions. I swam all day, hanging onto the flag and life preserver with one hand and kicking and trying to pull myself through the water with the other. I saw boats and ships in the distance and I tried to signal them, but they couldn't see me. Water got into my strobe light and it stopped working. All I had to signal with was the man

JIM & ANGIE GEORGE

overboard flag. By the night I was exhausted and tried to sleep, but it was very difficult."

He was thirsty and cold, and his feet were tired from kicking. He tried to use his arms, but he couldn't. He was afraid of sharks, and smaller fish kept nipping at his back.

"I tried to keep my spirits up by singing. I knew that it would be very hard for anyone to see me because of the waves and because I was so low in the water. The second night I saw the lights from Bimini go by. All I could do was head for Great Isaac. It was my last chance before being caught in the Gulf Stream."

Meanwhile, Christine had made it to Cat Cay, where someone heard her on the VHF radio and brought her and her boat into the harbor.

On the way to Great Isaac Cay there is a group of rocks called the Hens and Chickens.

"I knew I had to get out of the water and I started swimming toward them. I tried pulling myself up on the rocks, but it was very difficult because of the waves, and the rocks were jagged and had sharp edges. I finally found a place to rest, but it was very uncomfortable. The sun was beating down on me, and I was very thirsty. My throat was dry and I couldn't sing any more. My feet were swollen and bloody, and my body was parched by the sun and chafed by the life preserver. There was no vegetation on the rocks, but there were crabs. I was delirious and thought they were attacking me. I also thought that the seagulls swirling overhead were waiting for me to die. I was sure that if I wasn't rescued by the third day I would die there."

When Richard was about an hour into his story, Christine came over, listened for a minute, and then left. She told Jim that she just wanted to see what point of his story he was at.

"By the third day I couldn't swallow. My lips were cracked and my body burned by the sun. I couldn't walk on my swollen legs. I kept my bathing suit over my head to try to protect it from the relentless sun. I was sure that I was going to die there on the rocks and that my body would be eaten by the crabs and seagulls. I saw a few boats pass in the distance, too far away for me to catch their attention. I dozed throughout the afternoon, and then at dusk the sound of an engine awakened me. I looked up to see a motorsailer* that had just passed the rock I was lying on. I frantically waved my man overboard flag* and called to them, but they sailed out of sight around the rocks and my heart sank. Then they appeared again from the other side. The skipper later informed me that they sailed around the rocks to make sure that I wasn't a decoy for someone lying in wait to rob them, a common trick in the islands."

The captain of the motorsailer stopped several yards from the rocks and hailed Richard, asking if he could swim out to the boat. It was too dangerous to bring his boat close to the rocks, and even an inflatable dinghy would likely be punctured by the jagged coral. Richard said that he could.

"I dove into the water. It was a big shock to my exhausted and weather beaten body, but I managed to swim to the boat where there was a swim ladder. Two men leaned over the rail and asked if I needed help. I said no, I could make it aboard, but as soon as I got my body halfway out of the water I began to collapse. They grabbed me and hauled me aboard."

Richard's rescuers told him that Christine had made it to Cat Cay, where they were taking him. She and the boat were both OK. Richard had lost 10 pounds in three days, and Christine took care of him and nursed him back to health. A yachtsman from the local club paid for their dockage and gave them an anchor.

It was nearly two hours after he began telling his tale that Richard finished. We could tell from his intensity that this experience had left a deep mark on Richard's psyche. We wondered if this couple, on their makeshift boat, would realize their dream to sail across the Atlantic.

Little Harbor to Eleuthera

Angie: We planned to leave Little Harbor for the Exumas on St. Patrick's Day. Because we wanted to get an early start and didn't want to be held up waiting for the tide, we anchored the day before at Lynard Cay, just outside Little Harbor and close to the Little Harbor Passage out to the ocean. We spent much of the day changing anchorages because the wind kept switching.

The next morning, the waves were crashing on the reefs in Little Harbor Passage. We had been told to keep on a course of 330 aiming for Little Harbor Light to clear the reefs. We guided *Escapade* through the passage at six o'clock with our hearts pounding. Soon we were off soundings (the water too deep for our depth sounder to measure it). By nine we were sailing in force five wind (twenty knots or so) on a broad reach in four to eight foot waves with reefed main and our small jib* up. The wind blowing the tops off the waves made it an exhilarating sail, with nothing around us but ocean and blue sky, but fortunately the seas were with us. Once in a while we would catch a surf and watch the speed gauge top seven knots, above *Escapade*'s theoretical maximum hull speed. We changed places on the tiller every hour and a half or so, partly because it was so much fun, and partly because helming the boat in these conditions was tiring mentally and physically. By 1415 (a quarter past two p.m.) We had arrived at Royal Island, a distance of 55 nautical miles from Little Harbor Passage, at an average speed of 6.7 knots. That may not sound like much to nonsailors, but in a thirty foot monohull sailboat, it is flying! This was the most exciting day sailing that we'd had since our passage with Mike Carter from Block Island, Rhode Island, to Atlantic City.

We felt like we had arrived when we got to Royal Island, but it took an hour and a half motoring against wind and tide to reach the entrance to the harbor. You have to follow a narrow channel hugging the island on your left while you avoid the coral heads on your right. It was 20 minutes to four when we were finally anchored in the anchorage at Royal Island. We'd expected to find a quiet anchorage, but it was rock and roll all night long. We found that once we left the Abacos, fully protected anchorages were rare. You usually had to pick a spot depending on the wind at the time, and if it shifted you either rode it out uncomfortably or found a new spot to anchor,

The highlight of our visit to Eleuthera was Spanish Wells, a lovely little town, where we hoped to celebrate Jim's fiftieth birthday. Unfortunately this was one of the rare times when Jim had an upset stomach and didn't feel up to par. The houses, with their arch shaped windows, have a Spanish flavor. They are painted in bright colors—lime green, burnt orange, bright yellow—and most have yards filled with hibiscus and other beautiful flowers. It is an all-white community and the blacks who work there return to their homes on another part of the island at night. Later we saw the stark contrast between the two communities. The island is much hillier than the Abacos and much busier. Traffic in the harbor is heavy with small motorboats zooming around at wide open speed, and they drove their cars the same way in town. One afternoon we noticed people on shore all staring into the water. A tow truck was letting its hoist down into the water and soon it was pulling a yellow Datsun out. Its owner had parked too close to the edge of the wharf and not set his brake. The crowd watching the recovery was laughing and enjoying the spectacle. Before leaving Spanish Wells we filled up our four five gallon jerry cans and our thirty gallon water tank with fresh water. We didn't know when we would get fresh water again.

We were in a hurry to get to the Exumas, so as soon as the weather seemed favorable we set out for Hatchet Bay. Hatchet Bay was only a short sail from Spanish Wells but we couldn't leave until one thirty in the afternoon because we needed a slack tide to make it through Current Cut. Once past the cut, the water is real shallow. You have to make a right turn as soon as you pass the rocks at the end of the cut and then hug the starboard shore. The weather had seemed perfect for a sail in the harbor at Spanish Wells, but once we were out on the ocean, we found that the wind was blowing 25 to 30 knots. Luckily our destination was downwind, and we sailed along under double reefed main averaging five knots, admiring the high limestone cliffs as we passed. What a contrast to the low lying islands of the Abacos. It was about five o'clock when we neared Hatchet Bay and began scanning the cliffs for the entrance to the harbor. We were a little anxious, because the sun goes down in the tropics at six, and dark comes almost immediately. We finally spotted the silos we had been told were near the entrance to the harbor, and then the harbor entrance itself.

We had heard that Alice Town in Hatchet Bay had the best ice cream in the Bahamas, so the next afternoon we decided to go ashore and find the town. Alice Town was a stark contrast to Spanish Wells. While Spanish Wells was an all-white town and obviously prosperous, Alice Town was all black and the town mirrored differences in the the economic level of the two groups. The unpainted somewhat dilapidated houses, some only shacks with no windows, rusted cars and the kids in the schoolyard playing basketball without a hoop reminded Angie of when she taught in Phenix City, Alabama, in the Sixties. We asked a young lady where we could buy produce and ice cream. She seemed reluctant to talk to us, but she gave us some directions. Everyone else we encountered in the village was friendly. We found the packing house where produce was being packed in cartons to be distributed to other islands. After picking our produce from the boxes we paid a dollar and a half for two green, two red, and two goat (hot) peppers, a pineapple and a bunch of bananas. Next we found the dairy and walked around trying to figure out how to get in. After we spotted someone through a window and yelled to him, he led us into the place and showed us the ice cream. We could see that we weren't going to get ice cream cones—they sold the ice cream in pints, half gallons, and gallons—so we bought a pint of strawberry and a pint of rum raisin. Since we didn't have a freezer to keep it in on *Escapade*, we devoured both pints. It was rich and creamy, tasting the way we remember ice cream tasting when we were kids.

Our last stop before leaving Eleuthera for the Exumas was at the Cape Eleuthera Marina. The marina itself was closed down, but boats were still going in to anchor or tie up at the dock. Shortly after we anchored, a sport fishing boat, the *Black C*, came into the harbor and tied up. When we saw the crew cleaning fish on the dock, we climbed into the dinghy and headed over to see if we could buy some. There were no ladders, so we tied off to a boat and Jim climbed up on the dock. The captain of the *Black C* wanted me to see all of the dorado (mahi mahi) that he had caught, so Jim helped me up onto the dock, a long stretch for my legs. There were about ten huge dorado lying on the dock. While you could still see some yellow on their bodies, there was nothing like the brilliant color they display when they jump out of the water at the end of your fishing line. Cap gave us a dorado filet and four wahoo steaks. The wahoo, he said, was a great tasting fish, but you can't buy it in the states because it doesn't transport well. We were thrilled to get it!

Back on *Escapade*, we saw a Bahamian talking to the people whose boats were at the dock. We figured that he was "unofficially" collecting the $5.00 that the marina had charged people to tie at the dock before it closed down. When he yelled at us that we couldn't anchor but had to tie up at the dock, Jim got in the dinghy and went ashore to negotiate with him. He told him that we had heard that it cost $2.00 to anchor in the bay. The "dockmaster" asked Jim if he had three dollars. Jim gave it to him and came back to the boat.

The Exuma Islands

Most sailors who visit the Bahamas every year head for the Exuma Islands, and it's easy so see why. Even though the anchorages are less protected than in the Abacos (which makes the Abacos easier for neophyte cruisers), the Exumas offer one beautiful anchorage after another. You really get the feeling of exploring a tropical paradise, and you can often find your own little spot in paradise for a night or two, or at least this was true in 1986 when we were there on *Escapade*. This is what people imagine when they dream of the cruising life.

One of our first stops in the Exumas was Alan Cay, noted mainly for a species of iguanas not found anywhere else in the world. We anchored *Escapade* and took the dinghy ashore to visit a beautiful beach laced with palm trees backed by a formidable looking tropical forest. About twenty-five or thirty iguanas of various sizes up to three feet long were scattered up and down the beach. We decided that this would be a good place to clean the bottom of our dinghy, which had grown a beard of slimy green moss. We flipped it over and as we scraped away at the bottom, the iguanas began to converge on us. They seemed to be curious about us and our activity. We were a little nervous as some of the bigger ones got close to us, but we had read that they were vegetarian and not prone to attack. They were really quite beautiful in a primeval kind of way with their spiny backs and scaly loose-fitting skin and the blue patches on their heads. We could imagine ourselves transported in a time machine into a prehuman world where dinosaurs might emerge from the forest at any moment.

Angie: We arrived at South Warderick Wells on April 3, the day before my birthday. It has to be the most beautiful place I've ever seen. It is a national land and sea park. The waters are absolutely clear and every beautiful shade of blue from light turquoise to deep indigo. A wide sandy beach leads to gentle dunes where you can wander through every kind of palm tree and tropical flower imaginable. Our first night we were the only boat in the anchorage. We felt like explorers in a newly discovered paradise. (We understand that now there are moorings and you have to apply in advance to get one.) It was a comfortable, protected anchorage with only a mild surge, although there was a strong current, as there is everywhere in the Exumas. The next day one more boat, *St. Jerome*, a beautiful forty-five foot ketch,* joined us. We had caught a large grouper on our sail here from Norman Cay. We shared some of our grouper with the couple on *St. Jerome*, and they gave us two cold beers in exchange. We really appreciated the beers, since we had no ice and couldn't keep beer cold. The grouper, baked potatoes, corn, and the two beers from *St. Jerome* made up my birthday dinner, along with peach cobbler that I had made in the afternoon for my birthday cake. It was a perfect birthday! [Note: Unlike my birthday this year, April 2020, when Jim and I are confined to our house because of the Covid-19 pandemic!]

After a few days in this paradise we had to move on. We were running short of fresh food, and we were getting tired of the strong winds that had been blowing through the anchorage for the last several days. Staniel Cay was only a short distance away, but we had been waiting for the winds to moderate or change direction for a favorable sail. When we finally decided just to go and weighed anchor, we discovered that we had a problem. The shift cable that ran from the cockpit to the engine, which was located underneath the gangway, was frozen up and we couldn't shift gears. We finally solved the problem by disconnecting the cable from the engine and having me go below and use a vice-grips (Jim calls it the wrong tool for every job) directly on the transmission. We ended up motoring to Staniel Cay into the wind the whole way. After that I had to hurry below every time we had to shift from neutral to forward or reverse. If we were setting or weighing the anchor or picking up a buoy, times when Jim had to be on the foredeck, I had to go below to shift and then rush back to the tiller. I had the bruises on my legs to prove it.

We found a telephone station, a post office, and a grocery store in the village on Staniel Cay. We bought beer, carrots, onions, cheese and bread at the grocery story and then went to the telephone station. We wanted to call Jim's older brother, Chuck, to see if he could get us a replacement for our frozen shift cable (we knew it would be next to impossible to get one in the Bahamas without waiting months for it to arrive). We hoped to have our friend Dennis, who was scheduled to meet us in Georgetown, bring it with him. Making the phone call to Michigan was an adventure in itself. The operator in Staniel Cay had to call the operator in Nassau so that they could dial the call to the States. Then we had to go into a booth and wait for the Nassau operator to call us back. You had to shout to make yourself heard, and you couldn't always hear what the person on the other end of the line was saying. Anyway, Jim got his message through to Chuck. The call cost seven dollars. What a difference from communications today with the internet and satellite phones.

In the settlement, women washed clothes at outdoor pumps and wells in big tubs using washboards. Many cruisers paid these women to do their laundry. but we had our own method. We had picked up an old washboard at a flea market and did our wash in a bucket with Lemon Joy and hung our clothes out to dry on the lifelines.

Chapter Twelve:
Cruising Life

Jim: Georgetown in the Exumas is a major crossroad for cruising sailors. It is a first stop for boats heading for the U.S. from the West Indies and the Virgin Islands, and the taking off point for boats setting out on "the thorny path" to the Caribbean Islands (so-called because it is an upwind slog). So in the Exumas we got to hang out with full-time liveaboard sailors from Europe and beyond. People hang out there because of all the beautiful coves and beaches, the great snorkeling and diving around the reefs filled with colorful fish, the excellent spear fishing and lobstering for those who are adept at it (we weren't!), and not least of all, the camaraderie with other sailors.

While we were in Staniel Cay we heard that there was going to be a potluck on the beach. Angie made a pasta salad. We had to row to shore because our dinghy motor had conked out again. It was a tough row, at least a mile against the current, and we hoped that we could get someone to tow us back to *Escapade* after the party. We thought we were late, but the other sailors were on Bahamian time and when we got to shore they were still building a fire. Someone had caught a huge grouper and was roasting it over the fire. An overturned dinghy served as a table for the food we had all brought. After it was gone, we sat around the fire listening to two men from Germany, Karl and Mark, singing and telling stories. Karl was quite an entertainer, and soon he was making up crazy games, with the prize being a coconut with all of the boaters' signatures on it. Karl stuck a beer can in the sand. The contest was to run around the beer can ten times and then run over to a stack of boat cushions with the coconut sitting on top. I made it around eight times and thought I might win the prize, but a young girl made it around nine times, then ran over, sat on the pillows and crossed her legs. She fell off, but Karl gave her the prize anyway.

Norman's Pond Cay, Sunday April 13, 1986
[from Angie's journal]

"This morning we moved over to Norman's Pond Cay because the wind had shifted around to the south making the anchorage at Lee Stocking Island across from Georgetown uncomfortable. As we came into Norman's, I stood on the bow guiding Jim through black coral heads at the entrance to the cove. Jim found a spot protected from the wind to put down the anchor, and after a leisurely breakfast we put on our gear to go snorkeling. I was excited about that because I had been able to buy a new mask and fins at Staniel Cay, a mask that fit my head much better and fins that were as comfortable as a pair of shoes. Because the wind and current were unpredictable, we pulled the dinghy along with us in case we got separated from the boat. And Jim could put any fish in the dinghy that he might be lucky enough to spear. This was the best snorkeling we've had in the Bahamas. The coral teemed with all sorts of fish, red fish and blue fish and yellow and black striped fish. Jim speared one, but decided it didn't look edible and he threw it back. A huge barracuda swam up and was staring me in the face. We know that they are not supposed to attack unless you are wearing something shiny, but it made me nervous. I was ready to head back to *Escapade*. Anyway, it started to rain, and the wind was picking up, so we went back to the boat. We quickly changed out of our swimming gear and began getting ready to pull up the anchor and head back to Lee Stocking. While I was clothes pinning our towels and bathing suits to the life-line, I looked at the sky and knew that all hell was about to break loose. Since we were shifting from the engine, I asked Jim if he was ready for action. Just then the wind picked up and shifted, blowing us toward shore. As Jim was starting the engine we felt the keel bump the bottom. The depth sounder read five feet. This was the bare minimum that *Escapade* needed, and we were on a falling tide. I knew we were in trouble if we didn't get going. As usual I was at the helm and Jim was on the bow ready to haul in the anchor. I found out how difficult it is to steer a light sailboat into the wind when there are gusts up to 50 miles an hour. At first I wasn't giving it enough gas, and we kept falling off to port or starboard and Jim couldn't get over the anchor to haul it up. [The anchor holds the boat by digging into the bottom, and it has to be pulled straight up to free it.] We finally managed, and we switched positions so that I could stand on the bow and guide us out of the cove. Only now the wind was riling the water and I couldn't see the coral heads and had to guess at a safe route. We made it out, and when things calmed down, I noticed that the bottom of my two-piece bathing suit was missing. I got a kick out of getting on the VHF radio to tell folks that it had been blowing so hard that it blew the bottom of my bathing suit away.

"Only hours later we were back in Lee Stocking Island, the weather was calm, the sun shining, and we spent the afternoon swimming, reading, and cleaning the boat. I love this life and feel like I could live it forever. Unfortunately we know that we will soon have to begin our journey north and back to our jobs."

Georgetown

Jim: Georgetown seemed like one giant party, maybe because we arrived there just in time for the Georgetown Regatta, when sailboats from all over the islands had gathered. These were some of the strangest boats that we had ever seen, with crews of ten or more persons who seemed just as intent on having a rousing good time as on winning the races. We'll have more to say about that later. When we arrived in Georgetown our first priority was to stock up on supplies and to do our laundry. We decided to take advantage of the laundromat, but the equipment was in bad shape, with only two washers and one dryer in operation, and those were remarkably inefficient. At a dollar a load it cost us ten dollars to do the wash. We were happy to get it done.

The Peace and Plenty Hotel and Bar was the center of activity in town. Sailors gather there from all parts of the world. It was a major mail drop, so of course we went there right away to collect our mail. We sat at the bar to have a cold Heineken, a real luxury for us since we sailed without refrigeration. A young woman, obviously an American, was sitting next to Angie. Angie being who she is, they were soon in conversation. The girl, whose name was Maria, told Angie that she and her companion were here to meet and sail with some of his friends. That was Dennis! We were excited to meet her, and just as excited when we learned that Dennis had the shift cable that we needed. Angie wouldn't have to bruise her legs scurrying down the companionway to shift with the vice grips on the engine anymore. We spent the week enjoying having company on the boat, sailing day trips, visiting nearby cays, snorkeling and conching, listening to local bands and dancing along with the Bahamians at the Peace and Plenty. Dennis was a long time friend and sailing buddy with a great sense of humor, and Maria was eager to learn to sail. They both made excellent companions. Angie was in her glory because both Dennis and Maria liked to talk so there was plenty of lively conversation, or as Angie described it her journal, lots of babbling.

Dennis and Jim conch fishing

When we weren't sailing or swimming we were watching the festivities. These included a parade with a police band, the men in their white uniforms, some of them wearing leopard skins over them, followed by people parading and dancing in the street. At night there were always barbecues or gatherings at the Peace and Plenty. But the most thrilling part was watching the races. Dennis and I had both done a lot of racing, but these boats were different than anything we had ever seen. They were centerboard scows about twenty feet long with huge gaff rigged sails. When sailing wing and wing they reminded Angie of dancers with their skirts held out, blowing in the breeze. The sails would have easily overpowered and capsized the boats if it hadn't been for the hiking boards, planks that extended from the side of the boat out over the water onto which up to ten people crowded themselves to level the boat. The Bahamians cheered them on from shore. I"m sure that many of them had bets on the outcome of each race. We had heard that the Shark Lady and her all female crew on the *Barefoot Gal* often sailed topless, but unfortunately we missed that sight. When we saw them race they were wearing T-shirts. We would have bet on them for sure!

We were sorry when Dennis and Maria had to leave. We enjoy being by ourselves and have gained great confidence in our sailing, but the socializing had been a nice change from our usual solitary existence. [As we write this we have been living a virtual solitary existence for over a year because of the pandemic.]

The Georgetown Regatta

Chapter Thirteen:

Heading Home

At the end of April we knew that it was time to say good-by to Georgetown and start heading home. May was considered the ideal month to sail from the Bahamas back to the states. It was the beginning of warmer southerly breezes and before the hurricane season set in. The trip back to the Abacos afforded us the opportunity for more open ocean passage making. We were getting really comfortable with our passage making skills, trading watches three on and three off, taking sextant readings to plot our position, handling sail changes, preparing meals and and doing all of the other things that are made more complicated by bouncing along at six or seven knots in a small boat. We dreamed of a future when, with a boat better designed for ocean sailing, we could go off on an open-ended exploration of the seas. We took our time, stopping along the way for shopping and swimming, hanging on to what we knew would be our last taste of the cruising life at least until we were emancipated from our careers in five or six years.

Mike Carter, who had helped us on the overnighter from Block Island to Atlantic City, joined us in the Abacos for the trip back home. To our delight he brought asparagus, apples, nectarines, peppers, and New England maple syrup with him, all things that we had been missing while in the Bahamas. We were happy to have the companionship and the extra hand for our passage back. We spent a week or so showing Mike some of our favorite spots in the Abacos, ending up dancing until the wee hours of the morning to the reggae beat at the the Gully Rooster. We tuned up the engine, checked our supplies, and filled our gas tanks. Mike went up the mast to fix our masthead tricolor running lights. On May 23rd, at 10:15, when the tide was right for crossing the bar, we weighed anchor and left Green Turtle Cay. By noon we had exited Manjack Channel and were off soundings, headed for Beaufort, North Carolina.

Pirates and Drug Traffickers

As Angie told in her account of our visit to Mystic, Connecticut, we never felt threatened or in danger from intruders on our travels aboard *Escapade*. But there was one exception where, as Jim liked to say, we felt "a high level of concern."

Even though it was generally known that drugs, especially marijuana (which was considered a dangerous drug at the time) came into the U.S. by way of the Bahamas, we felt, rightly, that the drug runners were not likely to want to draw attention to themselves by harming tourists. And it's true that in some parts of the Caribbean, and certainly in other areas of the world where sailors liked to go, piracy was a real concern. But the Bahamas, at least at that time, were considered safe. Occasionally we were made aware that there was drug trafficking around. One clue was the presence of solid gray cigarette boats without running lights that left or returned to the harbor at night. And one night, while anchored in the harbor at Green Turtle Cay, we were awakened by what sounded like automatic weapons firing, though that may have been someone setting off fireworks. Another time we had found what we thought was the perfect isolated harbor. We were totally alone there except for the half-submerged wreckage of a small airplane. Shortly after we anchored and had settled down with our gin and tonics (correction, our rum and warm pineapple juice), a motorboat pulled along side and the operator told us that this was not a safe place and that we should leave. We did. Later we were told by some folks who knew some folks who had been issued a similar warning, maybe or maybe not in the same place, and had ignored the warning. In the middle of the night they were boarded by men in military uniforms and boots who ordered them to leave immediately. They were forced to find another anchorage in the dark. We guessed it was because a drug exchange was going to take place there.

Aside from those incidents, our months cruising the Bahamas were peaceful and idyllic. It was on our way home that an incident occurred that raised our level of concern. We expected the passage from Green Turtle Cay to Beaufort, North Carolina, would take *Escapade* about four days. It was our second day out, the wind was light, and we were ghosting along under sail to preserve our precious and very limited supply of gasoline. Nothing but flat ocean stretched from horizon to horizon. Then about four o'clock in the afternoon we noticed another boat far in the distance, slowly converging with us and then sailing a parallel course. When we got close enough we could see that it was a steel ketch, maybe about 55 feet long. It sailed along with just the jib and mizzen* raised, obviously under power and moving at our speed. Curious and a little nervous, I tried contacting them on the VHF radio, but got no response. After they had stuck with us for maybe a half hour, I told Angie that I was going to go closer and try to find out who they were. She said, "No Way, we should be heading in the other direction." My thought was that if they meant us harm we would not be able to outrun them anyway. I wanted to ease my anxiety by finding out who they were, so I ignored her. I started the engine and changed course to cross their stern. As we approached we could see four swarthy looking men in the cockpit at the stern of the ketch. I waved and hailed them as we crossed their stern, perhaps 50 yards away, but they only stared at us as we passed. I noticed two flimsy looking fishing rods, not the heavy ocean fishing type, stuck in the stern rail. Both Mike and Angie urged me to get out of there, and we headed off on a course which would take us away. We hadn't gone far when we noticed that they had changed course too and were following us perhaps a quarter of a mile back. I tried making a call to the Coast Guard to give our position in case we were in real trouble, but we were well out of range for the VHF radio to reach shore. As I mentioned, by that time I had "a high level of concern!" After a half hour or so, the ketch reversed course and headed back in the opposite direction.

Later, trying to figure out what all of that had been about, I speculated that the ketch was probably out there for a drug handoff and wanted to make sure that we weren't going to be in the way. A full moon made it a perfect night for a drug rendezvous. If they'd wanted to do us harm they could have rammed us with their steel hull and we would have gone to the bottom, another mysterious disappearance in the Bermuda Triangle.

The Last Leg:
Georgetown, South Carolina to Galesville, Maryland

Angie: It was great having Mike aboard on our return trip from the Bahamas, not only for the extra hand, but also for the stories we could tell along the way. We had some great sailing, flying the spinnaker or sailing wing and wing* whenever the southeasterly breezes gave us the opportunity. Mike and I were on night watch. We had set the mop and line up on the stern, hoping to catch fish. The clothes pin snapped and a wahoo jumped high out of the water behind us. Before we could haul it in, the mop went flying too, and that was the end of our fishing.

After a few days the wind failed us, and Jim began to worry that we were going to run short of fuel. In the evening on May 25 we could see lightning off to the northeast, and the weather forecast was predicting a low pressure area with Northeast winds and thunderstorms around Cape Hatteras. The shoals around Cape Hatteras are notorious, and though we had hoped to make it to Beaufort, North Carolina, we knew that we would have a tough time doing it. Cape Hatteras was the graveyard for many ships, and we didn't want it to be ours. So on the afternoon of May 26 we had a meeting of our three person crew and made the decision to change course for Georgetown, South Carolina. As we approached Wynah Bay a school of dolphins swam along with us, playing around our boat. We have always considered the dolphins a good omen, and these dolphins put on a particularly good show, criss-crossing under the keel, until one came straight up out of the water and down with a whack, and the whole pod took off. At three o'clock in the afternoon of May 27, after 450 miles of ocean sailing and 20 miles up the waterway, we tied up to the dock in Georgetown.

Mike had to leave us in Georgetown. He wrote in the logbook: "A great dinner at the River Room in Georgetown! Celebration of surviving the passage (never any question in my mind that we would) and a great way to spend my 32nd birthday! Thanks millions, Mike." It was Mike who treated us to dinner, and we had him to thank for helping to make our passage from the Bahamas one of the most memorable parts of our year aboard *Escapade*.

After a few days of resting up and enjoying Georgetown, we headed up the waterway. One of the luxuries Angie noted in the log was "A Bath in Fresh Water! Skinnydipping drew a crowd!" As we sailed and motored up the Intracoastal, now in no hurry, we took time to enjoy some of our favorite spots along "the ditch": Little River, Swansboro ("Would be a nice place to live" Angie noted), Cedar Creek, Oriental, New Bern and Belhaven, North Carolina, and the Little Alligator River, finally arriving in Norfolk, where once again we tapped our feet to the great Dixieland band playing at the Waterside. Angie logged "Great music, food, and people! Hope to return soon."

Back again in the Chesapeake, Deltaville and Fishing Bay, where we logged "some good R&R," on to Smith Island, sinking into the sea, where we again experienced the wonderful cooking of Mrs. Kitching, then to St. Johns Creek in the Solomons. We finally arrived in Galesville on June 22, 1986, almost a year to the day after we set sail from Toledo Beach Marina.

We dreamed of resuming our sailing life as soon as we had completed our teaching careers, but we knew that *Escapade*, as great a boat as she had been for us, was not the boat for permanent living aboard. She had been straining during the last passage from the Bahamas. We knew that a larger boat, designed for ocean sailing with a few more amenities, something like the Tayana 37 that we had seen at the Annapolis boat show, would suit us better. So reluctantly, we found a broker and put *Escapade* up for sale. Back in Ann Arbor we struggled to get back into the rhythm of a life that we had previously considered "normal," but the routines and challenges of teaching kept us occupied while we endured the seemingly endless Michigan winter. Angie's students loved hearing her stories about living aboard the sailboat, and their mouths were agape when she told them that she didn't have a shower for six months. (Of course she then explained bathing in salt water with Lemon Joy.)

By the time spring came and *Escapade* hadn't sold we decided that our summer project would be to bring her back home the way we had gone, give her a new paint job and some refurbishing, and continue sailing her on the Great Lakes. Before we could put that plan into action though, our broker called and said we had an offer. That summer we took up canoeing, and as Robert Frost wrote, "way leads on to way." During the next several years we did wilderness and whitewater canoeing, traveled in our van through all of the forty-eight contiguous states, all of the provinces of Canada, and most of the states in Mexico. We took up photography, making that a part of our travels, which extended to Guatemala and Costa Rica, to Morocco and throughout Western Europe. It was almost thirty years later that Angie said, "I really want to go back to the sea again. Let's do it."

PART TWO:
BEL CANTO

Chapter One:

Finding a Boat

Small World

Wednesday, September 19, 2012

I'm not sure how Angie came up with the page from BVI Yachts advertising *Small World*, a Westsail 42 sailing yacht. Not just any Westsail 42, but hull number 1, the prototype boat designed by Bill Crealock to be the ultimate world cruising sailboat. A year ago we had been looking at trawlers, dreaming of spending a summer or a year cruising the inland waterway on the East Coast. But we couldn't find anything that we really liked— they were too big, or too small, or too high on fuel consumption, or in the case of the one that grabbed us, the Nordic Tug, way too expensive. We told each other that if we ever found the right boat, we would fall in love and know that it was the boat for us. Then we sort of gave up the idea and made other tentative plans for the future—living in Italy for a month or two, taking a trip around the world, spending time in different places in Europe and the U.S. as the spirit moved us. Then one day not too long ago Angie called me from the computer. "Jim, you've got to see this!"

Small World was a beauty. Though she was built in 1974, she'd been lovingly cared for by deep-pocketed owners. And her present owners, Todd and Gayle, had spent 6 months refitting her, intending to take her on a world cruise. Then they decided that going into business together and building up some cash reserves for retirement was more urgent than world cruising. The boat had a new paint job over a barrier coated bottom, all new standing rigging, and every electronic device imaginable needed for long range cruising. She had a water desalinator, wind generator, and solar panels—making her, or the people sailing aboard her, self-sufficient. Everything aboard her was first class. Todd and Gayle, who are based in the Virgin Islands, had brought her to Florida to complete her refitting, and lowered the price from their original offering. We decided we had to see her.

We flew down to Vero Beach, Florida, and immediately hit it off with Todd and Gayle. They are the kind of couple you would picture as having spent their lives sailing—tanned and fit. They are a little younger than we are, but have children and grandchildren, many of them active sailors. They wined and dined us while pointing out all of the somewhat bewildering systems on the boat. I told Todd that if we were to buy the boat we would need several days of tutorials learning how everything worked. The next day we took the boat out for limited sea trials on the waterway. The wind was light, and although we had little opportunity to sail, we were impressed with how she ghosted along in very little breeze. Under power she was easy to handle, clean and quiet. Before we left, we looked at each other with the question on our faces—shall we do it? We left with the agreement that we would buy the boat if we could arrange the financing satisfactorily and contingent on the survey. The survey will be complete tomorrow. The financing is another story,

Cold Feet

September 22, 2012, Southwest Harbor, Maine

On Thursday we received the survey from Ed Rowe, and on Friday we found a message on our voice mail to call him. (In Southwest Harbor, with sporadic connection to the web, communications were slow.) The survey, except for one thing, was very positive, praising the condition of *Small World* and placing its market value at $5000 more than our offer. (Replacement value of the boat was $650,000!) I called Ed on Friday. The one thing he couldn't understand, he said, was why Todd had painted the bottom with an ablative paint, one that is supposed to wear away with the motion of the boat, instead of a standard anti-fouling paint. Ablative paints, he said, were never used on sailboats and trawlers because they did not work as intended on hulls moving at slow speeds. He did not recommend trying to remove the paint, since this would involve sanding down the bottom and possibly ruining the barrier coat that Todd had put on.

We called Todd and caught him on a bus going to see a doctor about cataract surgery. We let him know that we were upset about the problems we might have with this. Since it was not a good time to talk, he said he would gather information for us and promised to get back to us later. At this time we were trying to work out the details of financing a 38 year old boat—not an easy thing to do, we were finding out. As the day went on, Angie and I discussed our misgivings and wondered if we should withdraw from the deal. Finally, in the evening, I told Angie that I was feeling very uncomfortable with the whole business. She said she was, too. As we talked it over, it became clear that the source of our discomfort was not so much the bottom paint (which Todd turned out to be right about) as it was questioning our ability to handle a boat of this size, with this much sail and so many complicated systems.

Handling our Tartan 30, *Escapade*, had been like sailing a dinghy compared to *Small World*, a boat weighing in at 15 tons. Even though I once held a license for operating a 100 ton sailing vessel, the license was based on my knowledge of maritime law and my experience sailing smaller craft mostly on the Great Lakes. Angie was also uncomfortable with the speed at which all of this was taking place, and I could see her point. We had hastily signed an agreement to buy the boat after a very (for us) inadequate experience sailing her, taking her a few miles up the intracoastal waterway and sailing her back under very light winds. What's more, we didn't have our financing together and would have to take out a loan to complete the deal. That made us very nervous.

Finally we came up with a proposal that we hoped Todd and Gayle would accept. We would sail with them from Vero Beach up to St. Simon Sound in Georgia, where we were supposed to take possession of the boat, under their intensive tutelage. If at the end of that time we were not entirely comfortable with buying the boat, we would pay them well for their time, consider it a sailing seminar for us, and be on our way.

Understandably, Todd and Gayle were not happy with this suggestion. They felt, rightly, that we needed to make up our minds whether to go through with the contract or not. They were anxious to get back to the islands, (Georgia was in the opposite direction they would be going if we backed out of the deal) and besides, what we were suggesting was far outside the usual procedure for buying a boat and possibly illegal. With some regret, especially since Todd and Gayle were such great people, but also with relief, we withdrew our offer. We just felt that *Small World*, as good a boat as she was, was not the boat for us. Todd and Gayle graciously returned our deposit and wished us the best. But that didn't extinguish our dream.

The Search Resumes
November 21, 2012

We hadn't given up our dream of going back to the cruising life. In fact, we began planning in earnest how we would raise the rest of the money we needed for buying a boat, manage renting out our house, and provide for our nearly 17 year old cat, Sophie. The last was going to be agonizingly difficult for us. We'd raised Sophie, along with her sister Georgie (for Georgina) from kittenhood, and since Georgie had died a few years ago, Sophie had become much more attached to us, and we to her. But could we let our attachment to a pet prevent us from fulfilling a dream? We weren't sure how we were going to deal with that.

We forged ahead with our plans, selling *La Gitana,* our camper van that had taken us on joyful trips all around, Mexico, the Canadian Maritimes, and the southern and western U.S. We held a yard sale to get rid of extra stuff and to prepare our house for rental. And then we set about trying to find the right boat for us. The internet makes shopping for a used boat easier than it used to be. There is a great website, YachtWorld, where brokers from all over the world list boats. You can set the parameters of your search however you like—type of boat, age, size, price range, even the area where you want to look. Our first search came up with more than 30 pages of listings—a bewildering number of choices! Soon we learned to eliminate all the lightweight plastic boats churned out for the charter trade—the Beneteaus, Jeneaus, Endeavors, and the like. Since each listing contained numerous pictures, with Angie's help I began narrowing down the search to boats which appealed to our aesthetic taste. We were both drawn to a classic look (remember the Hinckley?) and so not interested in the overly beamy boats with interiors outfitted like RV's which seemed to be designed more for sitting at the dock than for serious sailing.

We soon found that there were a few boats, by a very few designers, that kept catching our eye—notably the Bristols and Valiants and a few others influenced by them. We made a list of the available boats along the east coast and in Florida and began comparing specs. This one has a centerboard (a long extension that can be lowered from the keel to give the boat better performance to windward). Did we really want that? This one only has a 30 gallon fuel tank—not enough for long range cruising. Then we began reading reviews, seeing what the experts had to say about the construction quality, seaworthiness, and live aboard comfort of each one. One important criterion was headroom. Since Jim is 6'2" tall, in some of the boats we liked in the 37 to 42 foot range that we were looking at, he would be bumping his head every time he turned around below decks.

We finally had a list of about a dozen boats that we thought might suit us. Most of them were located in New England, around Annapolis, Maryland, or in Florida. Since our search was taking place in late October and early November, most of the boats in New England had already been or were about to be hauled and winterized. We decided to begin looking at boats in Annapolis, thinking that we could take a winter vacation in Florida to look for boats there, maybe hitting Virginia, the Carolinas, and Georgia on the way.

We emailed the broker Richard Kahn in Annapolis and asked him about the headroom on *Outrageous*, a 42 foot Tayana listed in YachtWorld that had caught our attention.

Some of the designers—and all of the yacht brokers we later talked to—were short people and didn't envision six foot plus sailors clunking their heads as they tried to navigate below decks. "I'll have the owner measure it," he replied, and a little later the answer came back that it was 6'4". *Outrageous* was on a list of seven or eight boats in the Annapolis area that we were interested in, so we called some brokers, set up appointments and booked our flight.

The First Mate Speaks:

Thursday, January 17, 2013

Angie: Several years back I came up with the idea of buying a lobster boat and converting it into a craft we could live aboard with our two cats, Georgie and Sophie. I envisioned us cruising the Intracoastal Waterway along the East Coast, and perhaps taking it to the Bahamas.

We've spent a lot of time on the East Coast, especially in Maine, taking photos, and a lot of that time was spent in harbors. I was always looking at boats and talking about going to sea again. So we began looking at lobster boats and trawlers. Lobster boats seemed too small to go cruising in. We looked at Grand Banks trawlers, but I didn't like the design, especially the high bridge from which you pilot the craft. I also had a hard time listening to the diesel and smelling the diesel fumes. Not my kind of life on the water. I did like the Nordic Tug; they seemed closer to sailboats, but still there was the diesel. Anyway, they were way out of our price range. (Later I realized that maybe we discarded the idea of a Nordic Tug too soon. But that's another story!)

Every time we looked at boats, my eye would go to a Hinckley or some other beautiful sailboat. So why were we looking at power boats? We talked about motorsailers but I really don't like the design of that kind of boat—halfway between a true sailboat and a powerboat. Shortly after he turned seventy, Jim said that he thought he might be getting too old to go cruising on a sailboat. But ever since we spent the year on *Escapade* I've yearned to go to out to sea again. In my heart and soul I am the Water Gypsy. So now, Jim has decided he's not so old, and I get to go "down to the sea again" with my Old Man of the Sea.

The Decision

We looked at several boats while we were in Annapolis. One we would have snapped up in a minute, a Tayana 37, the kind of boat that we had admired when attending the Annapolis Boat Show in 1985. She was in beautiful condition inside and out.

Unfortunately, she had just been sold. Later, when we sat in the salon of *Outrageous*, listening to Grover spin his tales of sailing from Maine to the Caribbean, soaking up the atmosphere in the warm mahogany interior of the boat, we had no trouble imagining ourselves living aboard her. We were also taken with Grover, who had spent his life as a professional sailor. Now in his eighties and with two knee replacements, and also at the urging of his thirty years younger wife, he had exchanged the life of a seaman for that of proprietor of four coffee shops. He seemed like just the kind of man that you could trust to buy a boat from. Back in Ann Arbor we decided to make an offer, contingent on a marine survey of the boat.

The Final Step—Surveying *Outrageous*
Tuesday, January 29, 2013

Jim: The last step in our decision whether to buy *Outrageous* was to have her examined by a marine surveyor. In the event, this turned out to be Gale Browning of Hartoft Marine Survey. Gale has a fantastic history. She's sailed to nearly all points of the globe, and raced a 22 foot boat across the Atlantic singlehanded. She sailed her 65 foot schooner up the East Coast with her three children as crew, surviving a brush with a hurricane. She also took part in a cross-country motorcycle tour undaunted by a broken foot when she "laid her bike down" on it. It was a cold November morning when we met Gale, Grover, and Richard Kahn, our broker, on the boat where she lay in the slip in Grover's backyard on the Severn River. We boarded and Gale started by going over every inch of her deck with a mallet and moisture meter, looking for areas where the water might have permeated the hull.

When she was done with the hull, she went below and started going through every compartment in the boat, making note of the contents. She even insisted on removing some cabinetry so she could get a better look at the engine. When she was through, she sat down with us and made note of things she hadn't found. I don't remember all that she said, but the outstanding items were a fog bell and a book of the rules governing navigation, both of which were required by law. Grover insisted that they were aboard somewhere. It turned out that they were, but it was no wonder that she didn't find them, hidden as they were among the hordes of assorted gear and other stuff that crammed every available bit of storage space on the boat.

The next part of the survey called for us to take the boat the mile and a half down the Severn River and up Back Creek to Jabin's boatyard. There she would be hauled so that Gale could inspect the hull and the under parts of the boat. Richard said that this could also constitute our sea trial. I was too naive to dispute that. Grover started the engine and backed the boat out of its slip, a tricky maneuver since it required a very precise turn to port while going in reverse. What we didn't know at the time was that the boat didn't like to back up in a straight line because of the single prop and full keel. So many things we didn't know.

Once out in the river Grover handed the wheel over to me. There was very little wind and a favorable current, so we cruised along at about six or seven knots under power. We decided to raise the sails just for the experience and discovered that some squirrels had made their nest in the mainsail, leaving several holes in the sail and putting the kabosh on a proper sea trial. Grover immediately assured us that he would take care of having the sail repaired. (A sharper buyer would have insisted on a new sail when negotiating to buy the boat.) We also discovered that the self-steering wasn't operating. Grover and Richard both said that a new control box would solve that problem. This should have been a red flag, but I believed them. As it turned out the whole steering system had to be replaced.

With me still at the wheel we navigated our way up through the numerous boats anchored in Back Creek. Richard and Grover gave directions since Angie and I were completely unfamiliar with the harbor teeming with activity. The crew at Jabin's were alerted to our imminent arrival and motioned for us to bring the boat up to one of two piers, only with the bow pointed out. That meant turning the boat around in a space that seemed to me hardly wider than the length of the boat. This was a maneuver that I mastered after we had sailed on *Bel Canto* for a while, but I wasn't ready for that yet. I turned the wheel over to Grover, who adroitly spun the boat around and brought her up to the pier.

Jabin's crew backed the boat into the hoist and lifted her out of the water. After going over the hull Gale pronounced it sound but mentioned that there was some minor blistering. She said it was not serious and that we would find similar blistering on almost any boat in the harbor. On the way back up the river to Grover's dock, an alarm began to sound. Grover did a quick inspection and discovered the bilge filling with water. The problem was the stuffing box around the propeller shaft, which Grover solved temporarily by tightening it. He promised that if we bought the boat he would have the sail repaired and the stuffing box repacked.

A few days after the survey was completed Gale sent us her report, a 40 some page document detailing everything that she had inspected. She gave the boat a good report, pronouncing it fully capable of coastal and bluewater (open ocean) sailing. She did, however, also give us a rather long list of things that we should give some attention to— ranging from a cracked faucet to sticky seacock valves, to the need for a ground fault interrupter in the AC wiring. At that time almost everything on the list seemed minor and easily corrected. A few things, like the need to replace the dinghy, would involve considerable expense. When we called Grover about the survey he agreed to knock a few thousand off of the price and assured us that his protege Tyler would make himself available during the winter to fix most of the problems mentioned in the survey. We agreed, and our next step was to get the money together to complete the sale.

Finances

When we started browsing through the ads on YachtWorld, we began thinking about how much we could afford to pay and how we would get the cash together. From a little research we knew that whatever we paid for a used boat, we would need at least thirty percent more for incidentals. We were sure about two things: we were not going to sell our house and we weren't going to go into debt to buy a boat. We've always been savers, and by pooling our various savings accounts we figured we were about half way there. Once we decided that *Outrageous* was the boat we wanted, we reluctantly sold *La Gitana*, the van that had been our home on our trips throughout the U.S. Canada, and Mexico. We were still short, so we cashed in some of our retirement savings. After all, isn't that what retirement savings are for?

To complete the sale from Ann Arbor, we had to give power of attorney to two lawyers, recommended by our broker but completely unknown to us, and send them the full amount. We sat in the office of our credit union where we had stashed our cash, in command of more money than either of us had seen at one time before, including when we bought our house. I felt myself shaking when it came time to sign the order to wire the money to the Annapolis bank. Was this some horrible mistake we were making? I'm not sure what Angie was thinking, but I conquered my jitters and signed the paper.

Several days later we heard from Richard that the sale was completed and *Outrageous* was now our boat. Grover had agreed to let us keep the boat at his dock until the spring, when we could start working on it, and while she was there we could hire Tyler to correct some of the deficiencies listed in the survey. Meanwhile we set about having the boat documented under international law. We didn't plan on keeping her in Maryland any longer than necessary and didn't want to pay a sizable state sales tax.

Chapter Two:

Getting Ready to Sail

Getting Fit

Jim: Once we decided we were really going to do the cruising thing, I began pouring on the steam in my personal fitness routine. It wasn't enough just to keep moving. I figured I was pretty fit for an old guy, but I wanted to be sure that I had enough strength and stamina to handle a 42 foot sailboat. I upped the ante on the weights and aerobic exercises. I even went so far as to go to a physical therapist to strengthen a knee that once in a while felt like it might give out on me. This was all going very well. Then one day, lying on the mat at the gym doing some exercise which was supposed to strengthen my butt muscles (the therapist said this would help my knees) I happened to catch sight of loose, wrinkled skin hanging from the crook of my arm. My god, I thought, that's just what an old man's arm looks like. That can't be me! The sight was made worse by the fact that I had been going through slides taken on our year aboard *Escapade*, 27 years earlier. While I was never what you would call a hunk—I had what in my school days was described as an isomorphic rather that a mesomorphic build (you young ones, look it up!)-I still thought I looked pretty buff in the pictures. That image was enhanced by the fact that my slender but well-toned body sported what in those days we called a healthy tan. Ever since the day while walking along the beach in Barra de Navidad, Mexico, I started getting little rosettes on my arms from the sun, I haven't dared expose them to much sunlight. That, and the fact that I've already had a squamous cell carcinoma removed from one ear (ending my dreams of becoming a movie idol) means that I was going to have to keep my body pretty well covered while we re-explore the island paradises. Angie says that's probably a good thing.

"Little Did We Know. . ."
Tuesday, April 1, 2013

Angie: Little did we know what it was going to take to get *Outrageous* ready to sail and to turn her into our boat! We are in Annapolis, working 6 to 10 hours a day on the boat. (On the "short" days, we spend several hours running around Annapolis picking up stuff we need.) The boat hasn't been sailed for four years, and for four years dirt has been accumulating. I have never done so much cleaning, polishing, scrubbing, and painting, and placing my body in weird positions to do it all. We don't have to go to the gym. The boat is still at the previous owner's dock, in Saltworks Creek at Annapolis. Sixty steps lead down a steep hill to his dock, and we negotiate these several times each day. At night, we drag ourselves to our hotel room, too tired for a night out on the town or to play the games (Scrabble, chess) that we brought along to keep ourselves from getting bored.

After we bought the boat Grover had it shrink wrapped and kept it heated until we were able to come and begin working on it. And he's letting us keep it at his dock free while we get it ready to go to sea again. But Grover is a bit of a pack rat. He tells us he can't bring himself to throw away a bit of line (rope to you landlubbers), and I believe him. "You never know when you might need some!" And he had spares for the spares for the spares. He had prepared himself and the boat for extended cruising in remote parts of the world, and he wanted to be entirely self-sufficient. I'm pretty sure that whenever he replaced an old part with a new one, he kept the old, just in case he might have to piece something together sometime. It added up to 25 years of accumulated gear, spare parts, and junk. All well and good, but Jim and I wouldn't know what to do with most of the stuff, and besides we have to make room for our own things. Also, there were multiple books on every nautical topic and dozens of VCR tapes for a TV/video player. We threw out all but a few of the books.

So we've been up to our ears in work, going through drawer after drawer and locker after locker, sorting through stuff and trying to decide what to keep and what to get rid of. I never knew that you could store so much on a boat. The first day of this we got rid of 12 full construction size garbage bags. After a few days, it began to get real discouraging. But then we just decided that what had to go, had to go, and if we found out later that we needed something, we'd just have to buy it. Every once in a while Grover will come across something we are throwing out and say, "Do you really want to get rid of this?" Sometimes we keep it. We ended up carting away over twenty five bags of stuff and that wasn't all of it. Fortunately there's a trail from the boat up to the road. Grover loaned us his golf cart to get stuff up the hill, so we didn't have to haul it all up the stairs. But taking the golf cart up and down the steep trail is as thrilling as a carnival ride.

When we're not cleaning and sorting and throwing things away we are running around Annapolis shopping for marine items. We spend time talking and working with the people who specialize in some aspect of boating, e.g., graphics, engines, electrical work, dodgers (the boat's windshield), cushions, bottom painting, etc. It's real easy to spend money on this project. The old saying is that if you want to know what sailing is like, just stand in a cold shower and tear up $100 bills. We're finding out what the tearing up bills part is like. Only, it could be $1000 dollar bills!

We are getting daily inservice training on the mechanics of the boat, including marine toilet, diesel engine, bilge pumps, water tanks, refrigeration, and on and on. We have a crew of experts working on the engine, rigging, and the canvas. Our sails have gone to the sailmaker's to be checked, repaired where necessary, and washed. We've even had our 120 gallons of diesel fuel polished. And Grover comes around every afternoon, after managing his four coffee shops (and remember, Grover is 81 years old) to help us out. But too often his response to my questions is, "Read the manual." Unfortunately, most of the manuals are outdated. Some day we may even be able to sail the boat.

There are several things that have to be done that don't exactly take an expert, but they do take knowhow and time, both of which we have too little of. Things like installing a new water pressure tank or a vent hose to the cabin oil heater. Tyler was supposed to take care of many of these projects over the winter but had flaked out on us. To our great fortune, Grover introduced us to someone who has quite a bit of both knowhow and time. Rob Sutherland has owned boats all of his life and has lived aboard his boat for seventeen years. Compared to Jim, he's a young man (only 64) and can crawl into spaces that are getting a bit difficult for Jim. He's already helped us out a lot and will continue working on the boat while we are in Ann Arbor. Thank the gods for Rob!

We haven't tackled the technology side of things yet. One addition we'll be making is a chart plotter. It's a little screen, usually by the boat's wheel, that shows the nautical chart (i.e., map) and a little icon that shows where the boat is. Some sailors have actually sunk their boats steering the icon on the chart plotter instead of looking where their boats were in the water. Sailors talk about having a satellite phone to the tune of $1500 plus $50 a month for about 10 minutes of talking. Worthwhile if you are sinking, we decided that we'll just sink and not spend the money. We will have a life raft and an EPIRB that gives off a signal that tells someone where you were when your ship went down. I'm not sure who that someone is.

We're getting things under control, though. We can see the light at the end of the tunnel, and the boat will be beautiful when we get done with her. And we are having fun, even if we are exhausted at the end of the day. Jim says he never could have taken on this project without me. He says I'm the driving force. We're nearly done with this phase of our work and easing off a bit. Jim is out on the dock washing sheets (the lines that go to the sails). He says he will do the pillowcases next.

On our next trip here *Outrageous* will be taken to the boatyard and hauled out of the water to have her bottom done. There are a few other jobs that have to be done while she is "on the hard," as sailors say. One of those jobs will be to peel off her old name. *Outrageous* doesn't quite fit Jim's and my feelings about who we want her to be. The new name she will sport on her stern quarters will be *BEL CANTO*, Italian for beautiful song or beautiful singing. Home port, ANN ARBOR, MI.

And the Beat Goes On.

Jim: Things you should do before buying a 28-year-old boat:

- Get a thorough survey of the boat *and read it carefully.*
- Get a survey of the standing and running rigging.
- Get an engine survey

We arrived at the boat on May 3, with a load of personal gear and equipment, ready to start replacing the 30 bags of stuff that Grover had left aboard with our own belongings, a major step in transforming

Outrageous into *Bel Canto*. When we checked our messages before heading for the boat, we found one from David van der Spuy, the man we had chosen, at Tyler's recommendation, to check out the rigging. He informed us that he and Tyler would be at the boat at nine o'clock to do the inspection. David is a fascinating guy, a South African, slight of build and wiry, with a thick South African accent. After explaining to us what he was going to do, he strapped himself into the bosun's chair, attached the mainsail halyard to himself like an umbilical cord, and had Tyler begin winching him up the mast. Soon he was swinging around atop the 54 foot mast like an acrobat, calling notes to Tyler as he looked at every wire and fitting, from the mast top to the spreaders, and on down. He found several shrouds with broken strands, corroded fittings.

His final report was not encouraging. He recommended totally replacing the rigging, except for the headstay. That had been replaced fairly recently. We should have been prepared for this. Some people recommend replacing the standing rigging (shrouds and guys that hold up the mast) every ten years, and just about everybody agrees that you shouldn't trust it for more than twenty. From a safety standpoint the standing rigging is the most important part of the boat. If a shroud or stay breaks, the mast can come down. And in any kind of a sea, the mast in the water, still attached to the boat by all of the wires that did not break, can wreak havoc, even to putting a hole through the hull and sinking the boat.

The report on the running rigging was just as bad. The halyards which are used for raising the sails, and most of the sheets and other control lines, had been left on the boat while she had been in storage at Grover's dock for the previous four years. Superficially, they looked great. Many were comparatively new. But almost all of them had spots where they had been exposed to water and weather, and these spots were mildewed and in some cases rotted. Lines used for running rigging are expensive. They must be strong, but soft enough to allow the crew to handle them comfortably. Like the wire rigging, most of the lines on the boat must be replaced. Dave demurred from giving us an estimate on how much all of this was going to cost until he had worked out a plan of action and priced out parts. Our 3 a.m. worry that night was that the cost of re-rigging might exceed the value of the boat.

Meanwhile, we went ahead getting the boat ready to be hauled from the water for the bottom work. On Monday, the appointed day, Grover and Rob met us at the boatyard (so that we would have transportation once we arrived there with the boat), and we piled into the Honda and headed back to Grover's. It took an hour or so to get the boat ready to leave the dock. I wanted to handle the boat myself, but Grover convinced me that leaving his slip in the shallow creek was tricky, and that he should handle that part of it. As we pulled out, he demonstrated how by turning the wheel just so and gunning the engine in sync, you could get the boat to turn in its own length. From that point on, Grover stood by giving me tips on how to handle a 33000 pound boat, while Rob, the great guy who has been doing some work for us, helped Angie handle lines. The four mile passage down the Severn River from Grover's dock to Back Creek and Bert Jabin's Boatyard was easy. I just had to steer the boat in a straight line from point to point. We were motoring because the object was to get to the boatyard, not enjoy the ride. And the slight drizzle would have taken the fun out of sailing anyway. But I was scared nearly shitless when I learned that I had to bring the boat in between the two wharves, especially when the dock hands instructed us to turn around in there in order to have the stern facing the hoist. There was barely more distance between them than *Bel Canto* is long.

Angie: We'd called ahead on the cell phone to let the yard know that we were coming in, and there were two workers coming out on the wharf to meet us. They yelled that we had to turn the boat around. I looked at the space and asked Rob, "Can we do this?" Now you have to know that this boat weighs 16 tons. That's a lot of boat to maneuver—about like driving a semi-truck. My job was handling the lines on the bow while the worker on the dock yelled out what we should do.

Jim: Grover told me to turn wide but be careful because she pivots near the stern. I nearly blew it by turning the wheel the wrong way at first. But then I corrected and gunned it and she turned on a dime, just as Grover had said she would. The stern swung a few feet from the wharf on the port side. The guys on the other wharf, where we were heading were yelling at me to slow down, so I threw her into reverse and gunned her. The dock worker reached out and stopped her with one hand and the prop rotation pulled the stern over to port. Everybody said it was a perfect docking, done like a pro, but I knew that I was just damned lucky!

Back in Ann Arbor we received Dave's estimate for the rigging by email. It was bad, but not quite as bad as we feared. To make the necessary repairs and modifications to the rigging was going to cost $12,000, more than a third of what we had set aside for all the repairs, additions, and other expenses we had planned for in getting the boat ready to sail.

Wednesday, May 8

Angie: Another eight hour day working on *Bel Canto*. She's now in the yard, resting on her keel, braced by stanchions that keep her from falling over. So now we've traded a long ladder to board her for the 60 steps and Grover's steep trail. Yesterday we had monsoon rains and didn't get much done on the boat, but today is beautiful—cool, blue sky, light breezes—a perfect day to take the sails down. Oh, did we mention that the sails that we were so happy to get up the last time we were here had to come down again? Jim was awake a 3 a.m. the day we brought her over here worrying about how and when we were going to do that if it was necessary. Now we have some really big sails, especially the mainsail and the genoa (foresail). Together they would just about cover the floor space in our house. My trust level is really low, so when Jim said, "Let's take the sails down," I envisioned a gust of wind toppling the boat over onto our car, or worse, onto the two brand new sailboats next to us. Our million dollars of liability insurance wouldn't cover the damages, to say nothing of fact that we would probably be severely injured or possibly die. Jim is a good teacher and has lots of sailing experience, but did I really trust him that it was safe to do this? Usually I just dive in and do what has to be done, but I was really nervous about this. But I knew that we had to do it because we were leaving tomorrow, and the sails had to come off for the mast to come down, and the mast had to come down for the rigger to do his job.

Poco a Poco

Friday, May 24

Can you imagine us in a tropical lagoon, lying on the deck of *Bel Canto*, the boat gently rocking in the breeze, as we watch the the man-of-war birds swooping over the palm trees on shore and sip our rum and pineapple juice concoctions, the faint sounds of reggae from the natives wafting over the bay? Or perhaps ghosting along over gentle ocean swells, the white sails looking like a seabird's wing extending up over the blue hull, listening to the murmur of the wake as the boat cuts through the water.

That's not us. The boat is in the boatyard, on dry land, propped up on jacks, while her mast lies 200 yards away. Shortly after we arrived home from our last work session in Annapolis, we got an email from David van der Spuy, our South African rigger, that the mast was coming down and he was ready to start measuring for new standing rigging . (Remember, the cables that hold the mast to the boat and keep it from tumbling down?) We wanted to see for ourselves that all this was really necessary. We piled back into the Honda, loaded down with stuff that we will need if we ever do get under way, and headed back to Annapolis. The boatyard is sometimes facetiously, but accurately, referred to as "the dust bowl." Dust from boat bottoms being sanded before the copper bottom paint, toxic to sea life and humans, is applied. And dust from fiberglass being ground down for repairs to damaged hulls settles over everything.

Looking over the rigging, we were convinced that David was right about most, if not all, of it. The inner forestay, a cable that runs from the deck in front of the mast about 2/3 of the way up the mast and to which the staysail is attached, was half severed at the upper end. This stay isn't essential for holding the mast in place, but two of the shrouds holding the mast laterally had broken strands, and many of the other stays, while seeming sound, showed rust. We decided that the prudent thing to do was to follow David's recommendation and replace all of the standing rigging that was original with the boat. We hoped that when it came time to sell the boat, this would be a strong selling point.

Angie: We met Dave at the boatyard on Saturday morning to help him remove the rigging and measure the old to order new. If we hadn't done it he would have had to hire someone else, so we figured between us we were earning $25 an hour. That's better than we had been making.

Part of our job was removing the halyards (used to raise the sails) and topping lifts (used to control the boom and spinnaker pole) from the mast. These run up inside the mast, so we had to run messenger lines up as we pulled them out so that we'd be able to get the new ones back where they belonged. While we worked, we talked (can you imagine?), and I learned all about Dave. He is descended from Afrikaners, the Dutch settlers in South Africa. They spoke a form of Dutch called Afrikaans, and some of Dave's speech patterns and sayings come from that. For instance, he said that if we were to put an eye splice in the end of one of the lines, it would end up looking like a pig's breakfast. The Afrikaners hated the English South Africans, who they thought were trying to gobble up everything for themselves. Dave's mother is English, straight from England, so I guess his father got over the hating. It was fun working with Dave. He has an upbeat personality and makes us feel better about all of the work we are doing. He says *Bel Canto* is a beautiful boat and we'll have great fun with her when we get these major jobs out of the way.

Getting back to Annapolis enabled us to coordinate the work that still had to be done on the boat. We talked to Ann Miller, who was supervising the bottom painting, and Sean, who came out to measure for the new dodger (he's also making the new cushions for the vee berth*). And when we saw the mast down, we decided we needed all new wiring that runs up inside the mast to and from the mast lights, the radar, the wind instruments, and the radio/tv antenna. Some of these were undersized for the length of the mast, and some showed signs of wear and were liable to fail. So we got hold of an electrician and went over all the electrical jobs to be done with him. Chris Oliver, the engine guy, came and finished working on the engine, except for a few tests and adjustments that have to be done once the boat is back in the water.

Meanwhile we continued putting our things on the boat and trying to get it settled. This is really hard, because the vee berth in the forward cabin is full of sails, and the solar panel, which came off the dodger so that it could be measured, is lying in the quarter berth. These are the two main cabins of the boat, and it makes it hard to settle these areas. And the galley is still partially disassembled, because you have to take that apart to get at the engine. Everything that goes on the boat has to come up the 15 foot ladder. I must climb the ladder 20 times a day. I don't think I've been on a ladder that many times in my whole life before, but I'm getting used to it. In fact, I started cleaning and repairing a section of the rub rail that runs around the hull. To do that, I had to keep moving the ladder around the boat in addition to climbing up and down. It's no wonder that I'm exhausted at the end of the day! In my spare time (like when we're traveling back and forth to work) I practice tying knots. I learned some essential sailor knots when we were on *Escapade*, but I'm more into it now. Jim just taught me how to tie a clove hitch around a piling. He said that when I get really good at it I'll be able to tie it around the piling from six feet away, and that will impress everybody. I've seen him do it, but I'm not sure I'll ever be able to.

We have been taking time to relax once in a while, mainly by going out to eat. We discovered a great breakfast place, 49 West, that has the atmosphere of a sixties coffee shop. They have great coffee and excellent quiche. That helps us not miss our Sunday brunches at the \AUT\ in Ann Arbor so much. We also stop in at night sometimes for chocolate covered almond biscotti and cappuccino. Our favorite place to eat is a Thai restaurant called Lemongrass. They have a great happy hour—all wine by the glass and hors d'oeuvres for five dollars each, and their seafood dishes are out of this world!

Two jobs we still have to get done before the boat hits the water, jobs that Grover had promised to get done for us, is to repack the stuffing box and to fix a switch on the automatic bilge pump. The stuffing box is what keeps the water from gushing into the boat where the propeller shaft goes through the hull, and the bilge pump is, of course, what pumps out the water that does seep in. The list seems to go on forever, but we are making progress little by little. And we passed one huge milestone. Just before we left Annapolis, the graphics people came out to put the new name on the boat. And yesterday we heard from the Coast Guard that the documentation, which makes the name official and also certifies her as our boat, was just completed.

Chapter Three:

We're In

Sunday, June 23, 2013

Finally, *Bel Canto* is in the water and we are living (more or less) aboard. We were both excited to be spending our first night as actual liveaboard sailors! Jim was sure that he would get his first good night's sleep, without worrying about the next problem we were going to run into trying to get our boat ready. It seemed like every time we turned around, something new would crop up to delay us. Like when the electrician who was attaching all of the wiring from our newly rigged mast pointed out a through hull fitting, called a seacock, that looked like it wasn't seated properly. (A through hull is a hole in the bottom of the boat for water intake or outgo. If the fitting, valve, or hose connected to it fails, your boat begins to fill up with water and could sink.) He could move it with his hand. He said we'd better have it checked out while the boat was still "on the hard" (i.e., out of the water). So we called in Ted, owner of Seaside Marine, to give us his opinion. Ted took one look and began singing a requiem for drowned sailors. The seacock had been put into a hole that was too big for it, with 5200, a high grade marine putty, used to fill the gap. (Make up your own jokes.) It could have been okay for years before it began to leak, but then again . . . The solution was to take out the fitting, fiberglass the hole, then drill a new hole the right size, and reseat the fitting. This involved about five people and ended up costing us a whole boat unit ($1000).

So the mast was stepped, the through hull fixed, the stuffing box repacked, and we were ready to launch. The launching went without a hitch, with the owner of the boatyard himself towing *Bel Canto* to her temporary berth at the end of the pier. We had to be towed because Chris, the engine mechanic, still had some adjustments to do on the engine. We moved a bunch of stuff from our car, where it had been sitting for more than a week while we were staying in the motel, to the boat. Meanwhile, another Tayana 42 had come in and docked at the pier across from us. We went over to chat with them and ended up on their boat for "cocktail hour," (sometimes referred to as sundown g & t). When we got back to our boat, the alarm indicating too much water in the bilge was ringing. We checked the stuffing box, and instead of the two to six drips a minute that were supposed to be coming in to lubricate the propeller shaft, a steady stream was flowing into the boat. To top it off, the automatic bilge pump which was supposed to react to problems like that wasn't working, and the switch had to be operated manually. So we were awake every hour pumping out the bilge. We got a great night's sleep the second night, though. And last night we sat in the cockpit under the light of the full moon, on our new cockpit cushions, delivered yesterday, listening to music from our cockpit speakers, and cooled by the gentle breezes that had come up after a near 90 degree day. Even though we are still in Bert Jabin's Boatyard, we could have been in the islands.

How many does it take to . . .

Angie: How many people does it take to get *Bel Canto* ready to sail? Well, there's Rob, who has been helping us all along. Then there's Dave, the rigger, and his helpers, Tyler and Tom, Richard, the electrician and his partner, John, Mike, the diver, Ann, in charge of the bottom painting, and her two workers, Chris, the engine guy, Sean, the canvas guy, and on and on. Our count was up to twenty when Richard found the problem with the through hull fitting. That brought in Ted and his helpers, Todd, Brendan, Brian, and Benjamin, and a couple of others whose names we've forgotten.

We had planned to go into the water a week ago last Tuesday after the mast was stepped. Then it was put off until Thursday so that the electrician who was rewiring all of the instruments could finish his job. Of course, his job was made harder by the fact that all kinds of things had been added over the years, and much of the wiring was unorthodox, to say the least. Nothing obsolete had ever been removed, so the electrical system was quite a jumble. Then the electrician noticed the faulty throughhull fitting. So we had a hole in the bottom of the boat and an expected launch date of the next Monday. Some of the guys working for us are getting a hundred bucks an hour, so the old joke about a boat being a hole in the water into which you throw money and watch it disappear is hitting uncomfortably close to home. One of the sailors here at the marina says if you count boat units instead of dollars, each boat unit being a grand, it doesn't hurt so much. It seems like we get one problem fixed and we find something else that has to be done. I think about the Tennessee Ernie Ford song that my father used to sing—"Sixteen tons and what do you get? Another day older and deeper in debt."

It turned out to be a good thing that we didn't go in the water on Thursday. A Derecho came through in two waves, one in the morning and one in the afternoon, with wind gusts that we judged to be at least 60 mph. Todd had warned us to get out of the boatyard because boats sometimes toppled over in a storm. We took refuge in the bath house, in the men's bathroom because it had no windows. But Richard stayed on the boat, finishing up the wiring.

But now we're in the water and able to enjoy living aboard *Bel Canto*, even though we're sitting at the dock in a marina. Friday Tom (We'll have to tell you more about Tom later— he is quite a character) helped us get the sails back on. We figure we're about 90% ready to sail away, at least out to the middle of Back Creek, where we can anchor for free. And then we will be able to go out into the bay and practice handling the boat under power and sail. Hoorah!

Chapter Four:
Life on Back Creek

Thursday, August 1

Angie: We're still at the dock, but we've learned to enjoy living in our cabin on the water. We joke about having our vacation cottage on the ocean and talk about how nice it would be to just move it from city to city and experience living in each one for a while, then moving on. We are thinking Beaufort, South Carolina, Charleston, Savannah, St. Augustine. We could take that life for quite a while before we got tired of it.

After weeks of temperatures near 100, a cold front just came in and it's beautiful here. Ted is installing the new pod at the pedestal in the cockpit for all the new navigation instruments—a depth sounder, knot meter, and GPS, along with a new chart plotter that will show us where we are and what progress we are making against the background of a navigational chart of the the area we are in. That sounds great—and it will be when we are able to leave the dock. We're making progress, but it seems real slow. We keep finding new little things like the manual bilge pump (a back up for when the so-called automatic electric ones fail) doesn't work. We'll get there. Our dinghy motor conked out, so we're debating whether to buy a new one. I met a sailor on another boat who may be able to look at it and diagnose the problem. Ted said he would fix it, but he has other projects to work on; we don't want to distract him. Jim is sanding the bright work on deck, trying to bring it down to bare wood for revarnishing. It seems like an endless task, but Jim regards it as a Zen exercise. I will eventually help him, but it's not my cup of tea. I'm very content sitting in the cabin reading Jane Austen.

I spend a lot of time learning about the boat. I've learned to listen to the A/C to hear if it's running properly, the water pressure pump to know when we are about to run out of water, and the engine, to know when it is about to die because of air leaking into the system. (Chris is supposed to come and fix that problem for us today, but he hasn't shown up yet!) I've also learned to tie a flying bowline with two quick motions of the hands. Instead of going to the hairdresser or giving myself a pedicure, I make lists of what we need at the marine store and the hardware store. Washers, screws, sandpaper, work lights, tape, battens, inverters.

The inside of the boat is a mess because of the work being done. To get away, we hang out at a couple of different coffee shops in Annapolis and use the WiFi. We bought a hotspot device and internet service from Verizon, but we only get 5 gigabytes a month. We discovered that downloading movies from Netflix ate up too many gigabytes, so I had to quit Netflix, and now we're out of gigs until next month. We go to the movie theater instead. It's not the Michigan Theater, but we've seen a couple of good movies. *The Lone Ranger* and *Red 2* both had us laughing. Tuesday is six dollar movie day, and since boat expenses have put us on a tight budget, we take advantage of that.

We eat like kings and queens. We're discovering every happy hour in Annapolis, and there are some great ones. We can eat a dinner of half price hors d'oeuvres and a bottle of wine for less than we used to pay for a snack in Ann Arbor. Stuff like calamari, seafood egg rolls, crispy fried asparagus, lettuce wraps with grouper, Thai dumplings, avocado stuffed with crab. Cheap as it is, we can't afford to do that all of the time. We have been eating lots of seafood that we buy at the market. We'll probably start glowing in the dark from all the mercury. And Jim has learned to fry steaks that are almost as good as the ones he used to grill. There is a great Amish market in a mall not far from from the boat yard where we get good buys on meat and baked goods. We found another market in the same mall, sort of like a combination of Whole Foods and Arbor Farms, where we got some excellent produce and good coffee.

We're surrounded by wildlife. Not only osprey and cormorants on the creek, but I've seen a fox several times at night-time while walking alone to the bath house. Makes me really nervous because he/she stops and looks at me. Jim has never seen it. The other night we saw three river otters lying on a raft where our dock joins the pier. When they saw us, they slid into the water. They swam around looking at us for a few minutes to see if we were going to leave, but when we didn't, they did. And we've seen deer just outside the boatyard fence. This is all kind of strange, since we feel like we are right in the middle of the city.

Even though we've adapted to life in our waterfront houseboat, we are looking forward to the day when we can just take *Bel Canto* out into the bay and practice our boat handling. Our first experience leaving the slip wasn't auspicious. We had to take the boat just a few hundred yards to be hauled out again to have a through hull replaced and a new transducer installed for the new nav system. Leaving the slip, the boat got pinned against the dock, and Jim turned the wheel the wrong way to free it. The result was a bit of paint scraped off the hull. Ted's response, as usual, was, "We can fix that." There's a lot we have to learn about handling a 16 ton boat with a wheel, compared to our light weight Tartan 30 with a tiller. It's like going from a sports car to a semi-truck. I watch all the boats leave each day to go day sailing. Hopefully, we'll be among them soon!

A Great Day!
Friday, August 23, 2013

Jim: Finally! We disconnected the umbilical cords (the two shore power cables, that is) released our dock lines, and headed for the bay! We had adapted pretty well to this life on Back Creek. Too well. The longer we sat here at the dock, while Ted and his gang work on getting our problems sorted out, the more apprehensive we became about taking the boat out and actually sailing it. It didn't help that the last time we moved the boat, to have it hauled out for installing some of our new navigational equipment, I managed to turn the wheel the wrong way, driving us into the end of the dock and scraping a bit of paint off the hull. And that was with Ted's whole crew of four guys helping me and Angie handle the boat.

The list of things that should be done before we set sail seems to keep growing just as fast as we check things off. (Sailors we talk to say that at some point you just have to throw off the dock lines and go. You never do run out of things that have to be fixed or could be improved.) So we sit here, and we tell ourselves that there are much worse places to be than sitting on our boat in Back Creek. The cruising life isn't much different, no matter where your boat happens to be. But the truth is we get a little down spirited about the whole thing, and especially this morning when we got the updated bill from Ted (actually from Ted's office manager) and found that we had just about used all the money we had set aside for refitting the boat. Ted had taken off for a long weekend without telling us, so we were sort of left hanging without being able to move forward on any projects.

Fortunately Ted had gotten the engine running reliably (it had been developing an air lock after running twenty minutes or so every time we started it up), and so theoretically we could take advantage of the lull to go out and practice boat handling. But did we dare? Neither one of us quite trusted ourselves to get our sixteen ton ship out of our slip safely, or more important, back into it. Then we had a brainstorm. Tom Yoho. Tom, who lives on his boat here at Jabin's, is kind of a jack of all maritime trades. He does deliveries and just about anything else that people want done. So I went to find him to see if he would go out with us. He had a diving job to do, cleaning the bottom of a sailboat that, like us, had been sitting at the dock too long. He said he'd be happy to go out with us when he was back up from his dive.

So, finally, with Tom's guidance and help, we threw off our dock lines. We eased the boat out of her slip without incident and spent about an hour pirouetting around mooring buoys, approaching them from all angles, forwards and backwards, with Angie standing on the bow giving directions by mouth and hand signals. Then we headed down the creek and out into the bay. There was a nice breeze and a gentle chop, which *Bel Canto* plowed through effortlessly. All this time Tom regaled us with stories about the rich people whose elegant yachts he often worked on. "The wrong people brought me home from the hospital," he joked. After about a half hour watching the birds and the waves and the boats under sail, we turned around and headed back for the creek, our new chart plotter showing our position and our autohelm guiding the boat when asked to. Back in Back Creek we practiced once more coming up to a buoy, then brought the boat into the slip, with a bit of scuffling for lines but no real problems. Hurrah! a successful outing. Next time . . . we raise the sails!

It turned out that that we had been a little too optimistic about our engine troubles being over. We were still developing an air lock every time we ran the engine for more than twenty minutes or so. Grover had installed a double filtering system for the diesel engine. That's a good thing to have because if the first filter gets clogged by dirty fuel, you can employ the second while you clean the first. We later learned by hard experience what a good idea that is. But Grover had created his system by adding to the original one filter system. There wasn't room to put a dual filter where the original was, so he installed a second filter in a different part of the hold. That meant that there were fuel lines running every which way between the fuel tank and the engine. Somewhere in that mysterious maze of lines there was an air leak causing the airlock that was stalling our engine. After trying unsuccessfully to isolate it, Ted tore out the whole mess and reinstalled the original one filter system with all new fuel lines.

Wings!

Angie at the helm

Jim: Thursday before Labor Day was another landmark day for us. With Dave, our rigger, aboard we took *Bel Canto* out for her first sail. It was a perfect afternoon, blue skies, wispy clouds, and about 10 knots of breeze, just enough to kick up a white cap here and there on the waves. Angie was at the wheel, a big smile on her face, while Dave and I raised the sails and Dave inspected and adjusted the rigging. The boat felt solid under us as she cut throughout the waves, never heeling much more than 10 degrees. On the weekend we took her out into Back Creek a couple of times to practice going REAL SLOW, stopping and backing, and approaching mooring buoys. These maneuvers look deceptively easy but can be very tricky with a boat the size of *Bel Canto*, especially if there is any kind of cross wind. Then we took her for a short trip out in the Bay, doing some sailing under genoa (foresail) alone. Angie was at the helm, looking happy, while I handled the sail and figured out the course. We came back home and made an almost perfect docking in our slip. This is where the REAL SLOW is important. I have to come between two pilings and stop the boat while Angie grabs one of the dock lines and secures it to the boat and then reaches for another with the boat hook. I'm supposed to get the other two while she does that and between the two of us we get the boat controlled before she crashes into the dock or swings over into the boat next to us. This all went very smoothly up to and including the part where I bring the boat into the slip and Angie gets control of the first dock line. Then I'm supposed to put the boat in neutral and grab the opposite line, but somehow I leave her in reverse (used to stop the boat) and she begins backing out of the slip like a balky horse refusing to go into its stall. Luckily there was another boater there to give us a hand, and no damage was done. As they say, "No blood, no foul."

Free at last!

Saturday, September 7, 2013

Well, almost. We got up this morning in a beautiful little anchorage not far from Annapolis. Flat water, dead calm, clear blue sky, 64 degrees, a great blue heron decorating one of the docks on the shore. Breakfast of hot coffee, bacon, French toast. We sailed in here yesterday for our first night away from the slip where *Bel Canto* had been help captive for the last two months. This mini-cruise was a shakedown, both for our ability to handle the boat under sail and for practice anchoring, which we plan to do a lot of while we are cruising. The first part went beautifully. The winds were light, giving us a chance to practice our sail handling without too much stress on us or the boat. *Bel Canto* cruised along at about 4 knots in the light breeze, and we were delighted. Once in the harbor, our first attempts at setting the anchor failed. The anchor kept dragging through the mud as we put the boat in reverse and tried to get it to dig in. The type of anchor we are using is called a plow. For a good reason, some people say, because it likes to plow through the bottom, especially if the bottom is muddy. Thirty years ago it was one of the best anchors to be had, but today there are some new designs that are supposed to work better. One of them is called a Spade, and it is supposed to dig into the bottom like one. We think maybe we should get one of those. Anyway, we pulled up the anchor and went looking for a better spot with better holding. Angie was at the helm again, while I was on the bow spewing directions and handling the anchor.

Things did not go so well. The anchor is connected to the boat by a heavy chain that goes over a windlass (for you non-sailors, a specialized winch with teeth used for lowering and raising an anchor). The windlass has an electric motor for raising the anchor, and a brake for lowering. As you let the anchor down you alternately ease and tighten the brake to control its descent. Here is a short version of how it went for us. We chose our spot and Angie brought the boat to a stop. After the anchor got to a certain depth it stopped, even though I had eased the brake all I could. I gave the chain a tap with the detachable brake handle, and suddenly the chain was speeding out, landing in a big pile on top of the anchor before I could get it stopped. Not good. I started bringing the chain back up. As the chain comes up it passes over the windlass and goes down a hole into the chain locker. Well, most of the chain went where it was supposed to, but then it began piling up around the windlass. When I began letting the chain out again it formed a knot and wouldn't budge. I couldn't get the knot out by pulling it with my hands, but finally pried it free with a big screw driver. Meanwhile Angie was making a big circle with the boat. On our next attempt, the anchor stalled again, and again I tapped it with the brake handle to get it going, only this time I was quick enough to get the handle back in place. But while doing this, I accidentally stepped on the foot switch used for raising the anchor, and the handle spun backward and jammed against the deck. This time I was able to get it free with a vice grip pliers. Another circle. Finally, exhausted, we got the anchor to hold.

The good part of all of this was that Angie got really good at handling the boat in an anchoring situation (lots of practice!). I learned lots of things not to do with the windlass. We still think that a Spade anchor is a good idea.

One other big disappointment. We came here hoping to explore the creeks off the bay and maybe do some photography. But when we started the outboard motor on the dinghy it ran for a few minutes and then conked out. We're thinking a new outboard. Yamaha makes a nice little two and a half horsepower motor that we think would be just right for us. There goes another boat unit!

There are still a few little things that have to be taken care of while we are at Jabin's, like getting an exact measurement of the mast for going under bridges. The mast height of a Tayana 42 is supposed to be 64 feet, and the bridges on the ICW are supposed to have a clearance of 65. We want to know exactly where, or rather how tall, we stand. While we get this and a few other little things taken care of, we will try to get out on Chesapeake Bay a few more times. Then by the middle of the month, we hope to leave Back Creek, cruise the Bay for a few weeks, and then, in October, make our way South.

Chapter Five:

Cruising

Jim: We had hoped, and told everyone, that we were leaving Bert Jabin's Yacht Yard right after Labor Day. We moved aboard the boat on June 8th, and before we knew it the whole summer had passed while we struggled to get the boat ready to sail. We'd get within inches and then we'd discover another problem which would put us yards away from the goal line. Like the manual bilge pump (last resort if the boat was taking on water and the batteries shorted out) needed to be replaced. And the generator, which was so cranky and loud that Angie hated it anyway, was going to cost so much to repair that it wasn't worth while to keep it (I should take note!) We (Ted and his crew, that is) yanked it out. That gave us a lot more room for storing food and water. And the windlass, that we already told you about. Ted machined the faces on the brake, installed a new switch, and built new bow rollers for us, all of which should make anchoring a lot easier and safer.-And then the straw that almost broke our backs. We had never gotten the dinghy motor to run reliably, and the dinghy that we had inherited from Grover was sun rotted and beyond repair. A new inflatable dinghy and a four horsepower motor to power it cost us $6000, not one thousand as we had imagined. This wiped out the last bit of money that Angie had carefully reserved in our accounts. She cried.

But finally, on Wednesday, September 25, 2013, we took aboard all of our docklines. With Ted and two other friends, Gord and Karen from *Dancing in the Wind*, giving a hand, we eased out of the slip for the last time. The first leg of our journey was a short one, about 12 miles down the Bay to the Rhode River, where we are attending South Seas Cruising Association Gam. This is a big social event built around a series of seminars on all aspects of the cruising life. Most of the sailors here were heading south like we were, either for the Bahamas or the Virgin Islands. Many of them had been doing that for 20 or more years, so we expected to learn a lot from them. It was a great sight in the evening to look out over the anchorage where about fifty other boats, mostly sail but a few trawlers, were anchored and see the anchor lights, like a constellation of planets, over the water.

Anchoring, by the way, went off without a hitch, with Angie doing a great job bringing the boat to a halt at just the right moment and then backing down to set the anchor.

I must admit that I was a little nervous about the trip ahead. We had planned on the whole summer to get used to handling the boat cruising around the Chesapeake. But we looked forward to getting most of the month of October for that, before we headed down the Intracoastal Waterway. October is a beautiful time for cruising the Chesapeake with the trees turning color and the ducks and geese on the flyway south. That journey, stretching over a thousand miles from Norfolk, Virginia, to whatever spot in Florida we would choose for our hopping off place to the Bahamas, takes a couple of months. And though most of it is motoring down canals and rivers, there are some bays and sounds where you can sail and many quiet anchorages along the way. There are also places where you can "go outside" for a day trip or overnighter on the ocean before coming back to the waterway. Doing that depends on finding safe inlets along with a safe "weather window" for the trip.

After the cruising gam we went over to St. Michaels, a picturesque little fishing village and tourist destination on the Eastern Shore, for a couple of days. No wind so we had to motor all of the way. Well, I said we learned some anchoring techniques at the gam. We got lots of practice. First we decided to anchor in a little bight called Dobbs Bay. With Angie at the helm, we got the anchor set real well and had just got really relaxed when a guy came out on a big motor yacht and asked us to move. He said he was going to have to come too close to us when he went out later and then came back at night. So we pulled up and headed out to the main harbor, where we anchored just outside the channel. Again, we got what I thought was a good set and settled down for the evening. The next evening, though, I decided to give the set of the anchor a good test. We were interested in finding out how well the plow anchor was holding in the mud, so I started the engine, threw it into reverse, and revved it up. Well, there was a big jolt when the chain tightened, and the anchor came free. I waited a few minutes to let it settle down, tried it more gently again, and it seemed to be holding. I didn't want to pull it out again, and since there wasn't much wind predicted overnight I let it be. I wouldn't have done that, but I've got this great app on the iPad called DragQueen. DragQueen gives an alarm if your anchor drags and you move out of a radius that you have preset, so I set the alarm, and we went to bed. No problem, no wind. We'd swung 180 degrees but were still sitting pretty much where we started out. When we were ready to go and I raised the anchor I discovered why it hadn't held before. Our plow had snagged a Danforth anchor that someone had lost or abandoned. Good thing there hadn't been much wind, or we probably would have dragged again. Oh well, that would have been a good test for DragQueen.

October 7, 2013

Back in Back Creek, but this time at a mooring, not a slip at Bert Jabin's Yacht Yard. We came into the creek from across the Bay, after two nights at St. Michaels. We were coming into Annapolis just before the big power boat and sailboat shows were about to begin. This is the biggest boating event on the East Coast, and Angie, at the helm as we came into the harbor, was nervous about threading her way through all of the boats anchored in the creek for the event. She was even more nervous about handling the boat as we picked up a mooring, something we'd never had a chance to practice with her at the helm. We'd tried this before with me steering, and it hadn't gone too well, partly because when I was calling loudly to Angie, on the bow, so that she could hear my directions, she thought I was yelling at her. So did the skipper of a nearby boat, who came out of his cabin and asked if he could be of any help. Really, I was just yelling so that she could hear me, not yelling AT her. So we decided that it would be better if she were at the helm. And we bought something called the "marriage saver," a pair of hands free walkie talkie headsets. It required precision boat handling to stop the boat right at the big mooring ball, close enough for me reach down with a boat hook to grab the line attached to it and secure the boat. With Angie's practice anchoring at Rhode River and St. Michaels and my much quieter participation, she carried it off perfectly.

We took advantage of being back in Annapolis for a couple of routine appointments to get the new anchor that Angie has been wanting. Choosing an anchor is a religious act, and no one can agree on which one is the right one. But the one we chose, called the Manson

Supreme, one of the "new generation" anchors, seemed at least one step up from our plow. Ted helped us swap it out, not a simple task while we are at a mooring, since the anchor, which weighs 45 pounds, had to be attached to the anchor chain out in front of the bow pulpit. Twenty-eight years before, it was Angie who bought us the 33 pound Bruce anchor, considered the latest, best thing, for *Escapade*.

Shanghai?
Thursday, October 10, 2013

Jim: Almost ready to get out of Annapolis for good and start the long, slow trek down the waterway. Not much more can need fixing aboard *Bel Canto*, can it? So what happens when I check the gauge to see how much fuel is left in the starboard fuel tank. Empty? Can't be. I open up the tank and stick a measuring stick down into it. At least four inches left. Must be the "tank tender" gauge. We disassemble the tank penetration fitting, which works on a vacuum, and find out that three o-rings are shot. We call the manufacturer in Washington state and order the whole fitting, forty bucks plus forty-three for two day expedited shipping so that we can leave by this weekend.

That was Tuesday. By Thursday it still hadn't arrived so Angie went to the UPS site and plugged in the tracking number. According to the tracking, our fitting was sitting in a warehouse in Shanghai. How it got from Washington, via Kentucky, to Shanghai is a mystery. Many more calls to Washington and Lisa, at that end, promised to send us another, which should arrive by Monday. She was as mystified as we were, and as compensation agreed to send us an extra, since we are monitoring four tanks and are sure to need another at some point. Shipping prepaid this time. So we are here at least until Monday, which is not too bad, since the remnants of tropical storm Karen are kicking up a fuss here, causing a nor'easter which is taking its sweet time moving up the coast.

How are we spending our time while waiting for the weather to improve and our parts to arrive? Well, I just spent one afternoon and the next morning with my head in the head (toilet, that is), first rebuilding (with Ted's help) the pump for the manually operated toilet, because it was leaking, then replacing the whole pump because the rebuilt one still leaked. Not exactly the way that our friends view the life of liveaboard cruising sailors. It turned out that replacing the whole pump would have been cheaper to begin with, considering Ted's fee. The new one works a whole lot better than the old. That makes Angie very happy.

And since we are held up here for a few more days, we figured that this would be a good time to get our diesel fueled cabin heater working. The forecast of several nights with the weather in the 50's helped us with that decision. In the meantime a baked chicken dinner, garnished with potatoes, onions, garlic, and carrots, cooked in our oven which miraculously works without special attention, is keeping us warm and cozy.

Chapter Six:

Heading South!
(poco a poco)

Wye River, Thursday, October 17

Yesterday morning we dropped our mooring pennant, motored over to the fuel dock to fill our fuel and water tanks, and headed out of Back Creek for good—or at least until next year (knock on wood). All the little projects which seemed to be threatening to keep us in Annapolis forever were finally completed. The part for the fuel gauge which had been misrouted to Shanghai had arrived and been installed. The plow anchor had been swapped out for a Manson Supreme. And two big projects to add to our creature comforts: while we were waiting for parts to arrive, we endured three days of the miserable cold and rainy weather, which prompted us to ask Ted to show us how the diesel heater worked. Of course, none of the original equipment on *Bel Canto* initially works quite the way it is supposed to. Ted decided that the electric fuel pump for the heater needed to be replaced. After Jim bought the pump, we discovered that we needed a pressure reducing regulator (we sure could have used one of these last summer!), so that held us up another day. But Ted got it all hooked up, and now we are set to be warm and comfy no matter the weather. And the second big project. After disassembling and rebuilding, with Ted's help, the hand pump for the manual head (that's the toilet, if you don't already know), I gave Angie the gift of a brand new one. If you've only used a modern flush toilet all of your life, you probably can't imagine why Angie was so thrilled with a new pump for the toilet. Now we can flush with confidence.

Now we are anchored in Dividing Creek, on the East Wye River, Eastern Shore of Maryland. We are only about 25 miles from Annapolis, but it is a different world. As we came into the anchorage we were greeted by several great blue herons along the shore line and eagles soaring overhead. This morning flocks of geese, gathering for their flight south along the eastern flyway, lined the shore. We are the only boat in this small tree- lined anchorage which could only be more beautiful if the trees, which arjust starting to turn, were in full color.

Great Blue Heron in flight

Angie: This is what I dreamed of! Anchored in a beautiful, peaceful spot, the only boat in the anchorage. I remember the good times we had when we sailed *Escapade* in the North Channel of Lake Huron, the rocky coasts of Maine and the colorful waters of the Bahamas, and I longed to do it again. My dream has come true. There is little wind, a mist crawls across the water, and a bald eagle stands guard over us. What a magnificent bird. On the shore a great blue heron perches on a log just enjoying the peacefulness of the morning. The sun peeks out through the clouds, evaporating the water droplets on our cockpit cushions and dinghy. In my mind I am photographing all these visions, but in reality, I am just happy to be in such a beautiful place.

Anchor Watch!

Thursday, October 24, 2013

Jim: Sometimes it seems like the life of cruising sailors is 90 percent work and worry and 10 percent pure joy. We experienced a good dram of the joy on our trip down to Oxford, on the Eastern Shore, from Dividing Creek on the East Wye River. Even though we had to motor into the wind to clear the river and Eastern Bay, once we were out in the Chesapeake we had a fair wind and were able to finally make sail. For a little while we had a good breeze of about 12 knots and we were scooting along at six and a half to seven knots on a close reach,* *Bel Canto* was in her element, and we were all smiles and high fives.

We anchored in a small bight off the channel in Town Creek at Oxford. There was one other boat, a pretty Hinckley yawl, already in there, so we couldn't anchor exactly where we wanted to. We were closer to some private docks and the shallow part of the bay than we liked. The anchorage has the reputation of having a slippery bottom, but our new Manson Supreme anchor bit into the mud. Let's see, we're in 8 feet of water, and it's five feet from our bow to the water line. That's 13 feet total, and the right amount of chain to let out is five times that, or 65 feet. As the boat drifts back, I let out the chain. The depth alarm sounds, telling us that we're in less than our optimum eight feet. Depth sounder shows a little over seven. We check the tide, and it seems that we should be OK if *Bel Canto* swings to the end of her chain. Angie puts the engine in reverse and revs to 2000 rpm. The anchor holds. We're set.

As we were getting squared away and settled, a young couple rowed out to the yawl, waving as they went by. They boarded the yawl, and in a few moments, hauled in their anchor and left the anchorage. Now we had the decision of pulling up our anchor and improving our position or staying put. Out of inertia or laziness or whatever you want to call it, we decided that we were solid where we were. Even though there was a slight drizzle now and then, we decided that it was a good time to visit the village.

Oxford had pretty much closed down for the season. We went to a couple of boatyards, looking for lamp oil (our oil lamp does an amazing job of warming up our cabin a bit on these chilly mornings), bought a couple of spare fuel filters, checked at the small grocery store for lamp oil and bought a bag of our favorite Pepperidge Farm chocolate fudge cookies. Later in the day went back for a delicious meal at the Robert Morris Tavern, the only eating place in town that hasn't shut down for the season. When we returned to *Bel Canto,* we found that a small cabin cruiser had joined us in the anchorage. She was anchored down wind of us, in the shallower water of the bay. She seemed to be a safe distance away, so we climbed into our snug little quarter berth for the night.

I don't know what caused me to wake up at a quarter after three this morning. Maybe sensing a change in the motion of the boat or hearing the gusts making the wind generator hum. Anyway, I lay there a few moments and then decided I needed to get up and check things out. It felt like the wind was blowing a good 20 knots with gusts to 30 or more. I opened the hatch to the cockpit and looked out. The little cabin cruiser seemed closer than it had the night before. I couldn't tell if it was because we had swung on our chain or the anchor had dragged. I turned on the nav instruments. The depth alarm began going off, and the depth meter showed between 7 and 6 and a half feet of water. It was low tide, so that in itself wasn't alarming, but I had to make sure we were still secure. I put on my longies and a fleece jacket and went out to the cockpit. Off to my right, on the boat's port side, I could see the docks we had been wary of yesterday when we anchored. On my left, on the shore across the bay, was a brightly lit mansion. I drew an imaginary line between them, which passed just aft of *Bel Canto*. If we reached that line, I'd know that the anchor was dragging and extreme measures were called for. Of course, these things always happen in the middle of night. For a long time I stood with my arms outstretched like a cormorant drying its wings, checking our position.

By this time Angie was up and had put on some warm clothes over her nightgown. She started getting things together that we might need if we had to reset the anchor in the dark, specifically a spotlight and the headphones we use for communicating when she is at one end of the boat and I am at the other. As the boat swung back and forth in an arc of about 30 degrees, we increased our distance from the motor yacht, then watched it decrease again. I wasn't sure, as we drew closer, whether the decrease in distance was all because of our boat swinging on a longer anchor chain, or if we were dragging a bit. I started the engine, just in case. We spent a cold hour like this before deciding that we hadn't moved and that it was safe to go back to bed. By this time there was a red glow on the horizon from the morning sun.

Lessons learned: Have everything we might need in a nighttime emergency in a handy spot where we know where it is. This includes gloves for handling the anchor chain, pliers to open the sometimes balky shackle that holds the bridle to the chain, the handheld compass for checking the boat's position against objects on shore—and easy-to-don warm clothes! The good news was that our new Manson Supreme anchor had held.

Angie: I'm sitting in the quarter berth with a winter jacket and a hot water bottle getting warm after last night's excitement. I kept the hot water bottle and Jim from our last boat, *Escapade*. I also kept the 33 lb. Bruce anchor which I bought for myself. This time around, I insisted on buying a new one, either a Rocna or a Manson, although just about everybody tried to talk me out of it, and I'm glad that I did. I don't think this is how most people imagine our lives, but this is just another aspect of boat life. Where are those white sandy beaches, palm trees, and rum drinks?

The Way We Were (and are now)
Sunday, November 3

Angie: This morning we are anchored behind Fort Monroe, at the junction of the Chesapeake and Hampton Roads, about 12 miles from Norfolk. *Bel Canto* lies between bright red shrimp boats at one end of the harbor and a large dredge in the middle. We have plenty of room to respond if DragQueen should signal us in the middle of the night that our anchor has busted loose (we are being buffeted by 15 to 25 mile an hour winds), but Jim assures me that Manny, our new Manson Supreme anchor, is well dug in. Twenty-eight years ago we were anchored almost in the same spot. We had just settled in to eat dinner when we felt *Escapade* bump into something. Our plow anchor had plowed a furrow across the anchorage, and we had bumped up against *Deja Vu*, a Nicholson 33, fortunately (for us) well anchored downwind of us. Fortunately too there was no damage to either boat, and surprisingly we formed a lasting friendship with *Deja Vu's* own-ers, Don and Muriel, who became our on again off again companions down the waterway and in the Bahamas.

It was cold in the cabin this morning, in the low fifties outside. The first thing Jim did when he got up was light the trawler lantern. In less than a half hour the lantern had brought the temperature up a few degrees. We could probably get by with that, but we go through oil and wicks quickly and they are hard to replace. So he set about lighting our diesel cabin heater. First he has to go out on deck to install the chimney and open the air intake vent. Next he preheats the heater by pouring in an ounce or so of alcohol and lighting it with a tiny rolled up piece of toilet paper soaked in alcohol. After that burns down, he turns on the new fuel pump and opens the valve to let in the diesel fuel. A lot of work, but soon it's a toasty 75 degrees in our cabin. I think back to a cold Labor Day weekend in Maine aboard *Escapade*. The best we could do then was heat a brick with our two burner kerosene stove and hope that some of the heat radiating in the cabin would take the chill off.

My project for the day is to bake an apple pie, something I do at least once a year for Jim because it's his favorite. On *Escapade* we learned to bake bread in a pressure cooker used like a Dutch oven, and I made some stove top, deep dish blueberry pies. Now I have a state of the art (well, it was state of the art 25 years ago) four burner propane stove with an oven. The oven temperature isn't calibrated, but who cares?

Yesterday, after running the engine on our trip down here from the Piankatank River (I love writing Piankatank), we had a good supply of hot water in the hot water tank. Not only hot, but pressurized. So one of the first things we did after getting settled in at the anchor-age was to take a hot shower. Granted, this is a "navy shower"—wet down, shut off the water, soap up, rinse off. But on *Escapade* the best we could do was share two and a half gallons of water from our sun shower, when there was enough sun to heat it up. Anyway, our total water supply was forty gallons, compared to 140 now, so on board showers would have been out of the question. As often as we could, we paid for showers ashore at the nearest marina. Or in the Bahamas, we just went swimming with a bottle of Lemon Joy.

Now we have a refrigerator. On *Escapade* we had an ice box, which often went without ice, so we had to learn to keep things without refrigeration. It's nice to come back from the grocery store with fifteen bags of groceries (always in plastic bags to keep from bringing cockroaches aboard) and know that the fresh stuff will keep. And to have a cold beer!

Sailing seemed a lot simpler 28 years ago. For navigation, we had a compass, depth sounder, LORAN, and a radio direction finder. The last two worked only in some areas, and with them we could fix our position within a quarter mile or so. Not too great in the fog. We relied heavily on dead reckoning, which is carefully keeping track of the direction and distance traveled on paper charts, while correcting for drift, leeway and current. The autohelm connected to our tiller didn't work if the winds and waves were too great. Today we have GPS, a chart plotter at the helm, radar (which we haven't learned how to use yet), charts and weather info on the iPad, computer, and smart phone. [The radar turned out to be another bit of original equipment on *Outrageous* that was inoperative.] Our autopilot could navigate our whole course from start to destination if we wanted to set it up that way. It's complicated to learn how to use all of this sophisticated equipment, but we're slowly getting there. Of course, paper charts are still a must.

A lot of this technology requires access to the internet. Getting that to work has been hard, but we finally got it figured out, with a WiFi hotspot from Verizon, which is good as long as we are in the States. And speaking of the internet, 28 years ago our only link to the world at large was Jim's weekly talks with his brother Chuck via ham radio. We were blissfully ignorant of the news coming from the United States. Today we read the New York Times on the computer and the iPad, download books to read on our Kindles, correspond with friends and family by emails, cell phone, and, of course, our blog.

So I lie here in my warm bunk, feeling *Bel Canto* dance and sway in the wind, and I think, "Life is good."

Norfolk: Fair and Foul
Tuesday, November 5

Angie: Because the wind had calmed down, I thought that going the short distance from Fort Monroe to Norfolk would be peaceful and quiet. Wrong! I was steering the boat as Jim washed down and secured the anchor when I saw this big tugboat heading toward me. I changed course to avoid her, and she pulled into a dock near the entrance to the harbor. Minutes later I looked back and there were TWO tugs on my tail. The first was lashed to the second. Then as I look ahead for the next marker, this gigantic cruise ship crosses the entrance to the harbor. I had a flashback to being in the East River in New York City at the helm of *Escapade* with all the cargo ships, ferries and tugs and boats of all kinds seemingly coming at us.

As we got out into Hampton Roads we were in rolling waves. The tugs veered off and stopped following me and we made our way to Norfolk, passing the piers where the Navy aircraft carriers are docked. Twenty-eight years ago, as we passed into Norfolk, one of these ships was leaving its dock and hailed us with their hailer: "Sailboat, get out of the way. This is the Navy." This time they stayed put, but we noticed something new. Every time we passed anything belonging to the Navy, a patrol boat would be running parallel to our course, between the Navy ship and us. I wanted to tell them that we were the good guys, not terrorists.

As we made our way into Norfolk, I decided that I had been at the helm long enough—I wanted to get out my "real" camera with the 70-300 mm lens that I had purchased for the trip. It's a heavy lens, but I was able to hand-hold it and take photos in between waves. This was the most fun I had in three days. The entrance to Norfolk is lined with Navy destroyers and aircraft carriers, cargo ships, ferries, all types of cranes, industrial tugs, cruise ships both power and sail, as well as pleasure boats. This is a real working harbor, as well as the one of the biggest naval bases in the world, so you have to watch out for all of this traffic. As we made our way in, the captain of a huge cargo carrier leaving its berth radioed us and asked us to cross to the green side of the channel. "Then there will be room for both of us," he said. This, of course, put us on the "wrong" side as far as the Navy was concerned and brought out the patrol boats.

Chapter Seven:

Back on the Intracoastal

Coinjock, N.C., Tuesday, November 12

"The wind is blowin' harder now, fifty knots or thereabouts.
White caps on the ocean, and I'm lookin' for waterspouts.
Squalls out on the Gulf Stream, big storms coming soon. "

(by memory from) Jimmy Buffet

Jim: We are tied up to the pier at Coinjock (they sell tee shirts here that say "Where the hell is Coinjock?"), just fifty miles south of Norfolk. We had expected progress to be slow down the ICW (Intracoastal Waterway), but it was SLOW. After holding up for two days at Old Point Comfort, Fort Monroe for the winds to slack off, we finally decided that they had calmed enough for us to go on to the anchorage off Portsmouth, across the river from Norfolk. But then another mean mother from the North came through.

We didn't mind spending a couple of days in Portsmouth. It has a picturesque old town section (quaintly called Olde Towne), very friendly to cruising sailors. When we stopped at the little marine hardware shop appropriately named Mile Marker 0, since this is where the

ICW officially begins, and innocently asked the owner, Bob McBride, where we could buy some beer and wine, he offered to take us to Food Lion. (We had heard he would.) Like all harbor town grocery stores seem to be, the Food Lion in Portsmouth is located over two miles from the harbor. Not only did he take us but he offered to come and pick us up when we were done shopping and deliver us to our dinghy, all for a hug. Of course, we took advantage of this to carry back another fifteen bags of provisions.

When we finally left Norfolk/Portsmouth we got a bit of bad news. When we radioed a bridge about seven miles from Mile Marker 0, the bridge tender asked us if we knew that The Great Bridge Lock, the one lock we had to pass through on the waterway, about 12 miles down, was closed. The lock had shut down because of a malfunctioning valve, and nobody knew how long it was going to take to evaluate the problem, form a repair plan, and carry it out. This was on a Tuesday. On Wednesday we heard that it would "possibly" be open for a few hours each day, at low tide. The next low tide that would correspond with better weather and the opening of a bridge we had to go through on the way there was Saturday. A number of boats couldn't wait and left the anchorage to "go outside" around Cape Hatteras, a notorious graveyard for ships. Soon we began hearing the Maydays and calls to the Coast Guard. Five broke down, either dismasted or with broken rudders, and had to be rescued. We patted ourselves on the backs for our discretion. Saturday turned out to be a beautiful travel day, and soon after sunrise, we were on our way south.

But not soon enough. When we reached the bridge we found that it had just closed and that we would have to wait an hour for it to reopen. As a result we arrived at the Great Bridge Lock at about eleven o'clock, just in time to make the last opening until seven o'clock that night. As you can imagine, we were happy to make it through the lock, but we decided it was too late to go on to the next convenient stop, which was Coinjock. Not only were we beat, but we would be lucky to make it before dark. So, after passing through the Great Bridge Bridge (yes, that's the name) we tied up to the free dock at Great Bridge, a little way down the road. There we learned that Great Bridge is the site of the first Revolutionary War battle fought in Virginia and the first victory by the Union troops.

The weather was beautiful when we arrived in Coinjock on Sunday, sunny and about 60 degrees. Monday looked to be as nice, but the forecast was ominous. On our next leg we have to cross Albemarle Sound, a fairly wide body of open water, and then anchor somewhere along the Alligator River. Pretty much all cypress swamp wilderness with no marinas and no real harbors. And the weather forecast is for two days of gale force winds and temperatures dipping below freezing. We decided that discretion is the better side of valor. So here we are, tied up to the dock at the Midway Marina in Coinjock, sheltered from the howling wind and sleet (yes, sleet) outside and feeling *Bel Canto* straining against her mooring lines. The good news is that, since we are at a marina, we have shore power, which means we can have heat without using our diesel cabin heater. And there is a friendly little restaurant here that opened up just for us. The forecast is that after the front passes we will have four days of good weather, which we hope will get us down to Oriental, North Carolina.

Typical Days on the Waterway [Angie's Journal]
Nov. 18, 2013

We made it to Beaufort (North Carolina). Left early this a.m. and encountered fog in the Bay River and on the Neuse River. It was pretty nerve wracking. We had ½ mile visibility and used our chart plotter to navigate, but I still follow the paper charts and keep track of where we are. It takes two of us to navigate and watch out for barges, which are really huge. We were held up by the fog for three days in Campbell Creek, but I managed to get some great photos while we were there. When we finally left there was no fog. There were very few boats out today on the water compared to yesterday when visibility was practically zero. Go figure. But on the Bay River we had a hard time following the markers because we couldn't see them. We relied on our chart plotter and it was accurate. Of course, I was following the paper charts, but if you can't find the markers. . . Coming into the harbor at Town Creek in Beaufort was really tricky. You are surrounded by shallow water and we crossed one point where we sounded 5.9 feet. We made it, though.

Nov. 24: I was thrilled when I saw my first dolphin. I love those animals. It has been and is an amazing journey. Fortunately, I have Jim to share it with. It's my dream and he is helping me live it! It is challenging, and not everyone could live this life style. We will probably be traveling on Thanksgiving Day. Hope to celebrate it at St. James Marina near Southport NC where we are going next to wait out some more bad weather. It should be interesting tomorrow when we start out and the temp is 31. The winds have died down, so we have to take the opportunity to travel. There are small craft warnings up and down the East Coast, but it's going to be OK where we are going.

Running in Muck
Wrightsville Beach, NC Sunday, November 24, 2013, 4 a.m.

Jim: Did you ever have one of those dreams where you are running in deep muck, struggling to move your legs, not getting anywhere? It sometimes feels that way to us trying to get down the intracoastal waterway. I am sitting here at my typewriter (computer I meant to say—shows my age) listening to the gale force winds howl and trying to figure out when we can make our next move. We stayed three nights in a beautiful little anchorage called Campbell Creek, one day by choice, and the second because the fog was so thick that we couldn't see fifty yards ahead. This did give Angie a chance to get out her "real" camera and take some fog pictures, something that we always enjoy.

Three Fishermen in the fog at Campbell Creek

We spent four days in Beaufort, the first three waiting for the strong winds of another cold front to ease up. We probably could have traveled on the third day, but we were waiting for a package from my nephew Larry, who is handling business for us, and a replacement for the chimney of our trawler lantern, which broke because I let it heat up too fast. Finally last Thursday we pushed off the dock in Town Creek in time to catch the opening of the bridge we had to go through at the beginning of our day's run. It was a beautiful day, clear skies, warm compared to the weather we'd been having—a perfect day for moving down the waterway. We were feeling great. We even saw some dolphins swimming in the inlet where the ocean meets the Intracoastal Waterway at Moorhead City and that made us feel even better, as we consider them good omens. Then we approached the first bridge that was not a bascule or lift bridge, one we had to go UNDER.

You might remember us saying that *Bel Canto* has a mast so tall that we had to duck to go under bridges. That was a joke, but the official height of our mast, or vertical draft as we sailors like to say, is 64 feet. All bridges along the ICW are supposed to have a clearance of 65 feet. That's 65 feet above the water level at mean high tide, which is something you have to think about when you are sailing in coastal regions. Well, in North Carolina they like to do things differently, and there are several bridges that only clear 64 feet. And a super high tide can bring that down to 63. There is usually a gauge on the bridge where you pass through that tells you what the actual water level is. If you get it wrong, you can rip all of the instruments off the top of your mast, or worse, bring the mast down. We worried about this, so while we were in Annapolis we had Todd, one of Ted's employees, go up the mast in a bosun's chair with a long tape measure. I could have done this myself, and 28 years before on *Escapade* I enjoyed doing it. But somehow this far along in the eighth decade of my life, I was not so eager to view the world from that perspective.

Anyway, after taking careful measurements we calculated that our mast, including the instruments and radio antenna reached 63 feet and six inches above the water. Giving a six inch margin of error, that makes 64 feet, and we'd like to have another foot or so on top of that not to feel too nervous about it. Our first challenge was the notorious Wilkerson Bridge. Wilkerson Bridge is at the end of the 25 mile Alligator-Pungo Canal. There is no tide in the canal, but the water level does fluctuate when the wind drives water from the Pungo River up to into the canal. As we approached we kept looking at the water level on the cypress stumps and markers along the sides of the canal, trying to see if it was high or low. It was a calm day and the level seemed low, but that didn't keep us from being nervous as we approached the bridge. We knew that if we couldn't make it under, we had a four hour trip back to where we could anchor. When we got to the bridge we saw that the gauge read 65. It's best for your heart if you don't look up when you go under, but Angie did anyway. It always seems that you are going to hit, even if the bridge is 165 feet high. When we made it through we high fived each other, and I gave a big holler to release the adrenalin I'd been building up.

Well we weren't so lucky next time. As we approached the Atlantic Beach Bridge outside of Beaufort, North Carolina, Angie read the gauge and it read 63 feet. I wheeled the boat around, and while Angie steered I went below to check the tide tables. We were on a rising tide, a full moon rising tide at that, and by the time the water level would drop enough for us to go through it would be too late for us to reach our next anchorage. So back we went to Beaufort for another day. There was no room in the anchorage so we had to pay big bucks to tie up at the marina. Now Beaufort is an interesting little town, but we didn't need to spend another day there. Especially not a beautiful day for enjoying the sights along the waterway.

Friday we were up at 5 a.m., getting the boat ready to leave as soon as it was light enough to see. This time we made it under the bridge at mid tide with a foot to spare. It was an interesting day traveling through bays and sounds where it looked like there was plenty of water, but most of it was only two or three feet deep. The waterway cuts a narrow path where you have to watch the markers very carefully to be sure you are not drifting out of the channel. By two o'clock we were anchored in Mile Hammock Bay, on the Marine reservation Camp LeJeune. This was after transiting the Camp LeJeune firing range which is closed every other hour for firing practice. When we came through here 28 years ago, we were caught by surprise, stopped by a guard boat full of marines and told we had to anchor there and wait until the waterway opened up again. The current was fierce, and when we anchored, we snagged something on the bottom. When it was time to go a couple of marines in a launch helped us retrieve the anchor, and we rewarded them with a couple of beers.

There were about a dozen boats anchored in Mile Hammock Bay, and we all got to be entertained by the planes and helicopters flying overhead. We all left about the same time the next morning, timed around the first bridge we would reach which only opened once every hour. The rest of our day was spent trying to time several more bridges that either opened once every half hour or once an hour. If you reach the bridge too late you have to mark time in place until the next opening. That is not exactly easy to do when the current is trying to move you along at a couple of miles an hour. Fortunately we fell in with some boats whose GPS timed their arrival to the minute (if ours did that, I hadn't figured out how) and we could adjust our pace to arrive at the bridge when it was just about to open.

So here we are at Wrightsville Beach. Gale force winds are predicted for the rest of the day all up and down the coast. It's a protected anchorage and our anchor is dug in well, so we are secure for the time being, even though *Bel Canto* is rocking and rolling in the waves and current. Tomorrow might be OK for traveling, even though it is going to be 31 degrees when we wake up at 5 a.m. to get ready to go. After that we are expecting another couple of days of bad weather. We were hoping to reach Charleston by Thanksgiving, but at this rate we may be lucky to be there by Christmas. Are we having fun yet? The truth is that with all these stresses and worries, we appreciate every sunrise and sunset, every heron, pelican and dolphin sighted, every beautiful landscape we pass through, all our friends and family, and especially each other, more than we can say.

Angie's Journal
Nov. 25, 2013

We are at St. James Plantation Marina, a multimillion dollar development of houses, condos, golf courses etc. We are only stopping here because the weather really sucks. It was 31 this morning when we started out at 7:30. I had long underwear and several layers and still was freezing my butt off, and Jim had to be extra careful in bringing up the anchor because the deck was icy. Now we are plugged into shore power and have heat.

While here we played a game of chess to pass the time. I'd rather play Scrabble, but I beat Jim at chess once in a while when he makes mistakes. We really haven't had time to play Scrabble or chess because we go to bed early so that we can get up at 5:00 to get ready to travel down the ICW. The weather is 15-25 degrees below normal for this time of the year. When we traveled this same route 28 years ago, a couple of weeks earlier in November, it was beautiful.

Captain Braveheart
Sunday, December 1, 2013

Jim: Angie has been promoted from First Mate to Co-Captain. Not only that, but she has been awarded the appellation "Captain Braveheart" for stellar performance beyond the call of duty. How did this come about? There are several stretches along the ICW that the guide books list as "ICW trouble spots." To understand this, you have to know that the ICW is a hodgepodge of waterways made up of canals connecting rivers, bays, and sounds. So you can be motoring (almost always motoring unless you are extremely lucky to catch the right combination of room to maneuver, wind direction, and current) along a narrow ditch, next crossing a large sound that looks like it has plenty of water but only a narrow band of it is deep enough to accommodate anything but a canoe, then heading down (or up) a river being pushed along or bucked by a swift current. Along the way there are fixed bridges that, in our case, have to be timed for clearance, bascule and swing bridges with set opening times that we have to plan for.

This whole system has a "project depth" of 12 feet, which means that at low tide (or what is officially called mean lower low water) there should be at least 6 feet of water under our keel, and the bridges are supposed to have a minimum of 65 foot clearance at high water, while we need a minimum of 64. But then there is the reality, and hence the "ICW trouble spots." For example, a couple of days ago we passed through a section of the waterway affectionately called The Rock Pile by boaters. This is how it is described on the official NOAA charts: "Numerous rock ledges have been reported abutting the deep portion of the Intracoastal Waterway channel from Nixon Crossroads to Latitude 33.42.51N. Mariners should use extreme caution in this area." The narrowest and rockiest stretch is called "The Rock Pile." Narrow means that if we happened to meet a tug in this area, one of us might have to go into the rocks to avoid a collision.

In the past when we came to difficult areas Angie has passed the wheel off to me, but she was steering when we came to the Rock Pile and showed no interest in relinquishing command. In fact, she had a look on her face that said, "What's so hard about this?" It must have been her experience avoiding the rocks while whitewater canoeing that gave her such confidence. Anyway there was nothing left for this Nervous Nelly of a captain to do but go up on the foredeck and pretend to be helping us to avoid obstacles. Then there was was the Lafayette Bridge. In North Carolina, where there are several bridges with clearances reportedly less than 65 feet, most of the bridges have gauges which show the water level. But in South Carolina they have dispensed with that nicety. Also, in South Carolina, the tides are greater and the currents swifter. So as we approached the Lafayette Bridge, we were racing along at about 9 and a half miles an hour. That may not sound like racing to you, but it is 50 percent above our normal cruising speed, and faster than the boat is theoretically capable of going according to some complicated calculation that only naval architects understand. And the fact that the current was sweeping us toward the bridge was not a good thing in case at the last moment we decided we would not clear. As we approached, we watched the water level on all of the markers and pilings we passed, trying to see how much the tide had fallen from high tide. It appeared that the water was down about a foot. Of course, there was no gauge on the bridge to verify this, but Angie lined *Bel Canto* up and charged through the narrow space between the bridge stanchions like she was running a chute between rocks on a whitewater rapids.

There are the trouble spots where "frequent shoaling has been reported in this area." These are usually places where the waterway crosses inlets from the ocean, or where you are transversing a river delta. Then the usual reading of 10 or 12 or above on our depth sounder can quickly drop to 7 or 6 or even 5. I guess this is why they call it *mean* low water. So again, we try to cross these at mid or high tide, but that isn't always enough. Angie was guiding *Bel Canto* through one of these spots when the depth began to drop. It was above "lower low water," so I said, "Keep your courage up, Angie." She did a great job of getting us through, although the alarm on our depth sounder kept going off. Ever since then, when we hit a low spot, she says, "I'm keeping my courage up!" and she does.

So what makes the stress, and getting up at 5 a.m. on frigid mornings to make use of the limited daylight, worth it? For the last three or four days we have passed through some beautiful scenery. Cypress swamps and savannahs and low sand dunes. And we've spent our nights in delightful anchorages. Yesterday we saw two bald eagles resting atop a dead tree as we left our anchorage, and today, several times we spotted dolphins fishing along the edge of the channel. Every day there is something new to experience. One thing sure, we are never bored.

Angie's Journal
Dec. 2, 2013

We anchored just before reaching Charleston in a 7 ft. tide which is very high for this area. We had to wait for the tide to go down so that we could get under the Isle of Palms Bridge, before Charleston. Dolphins were swimming around the boat this a.m. The good thing about the high tide is that I didn't have to get up at 5:00 a.m. this morning. Just after Charleston we had to pass through Elliott Cut. It is narrow, broken rock on both sides, and the current runs up to five knots through it. We misjudged and we entered the cut with the current against us. It took us almost a half hour to go a half mile. At times we seemed not to be moving at all, and all I could think of was what a terrible time it would be to have an engine failure!

We are going to find a place to stop for a while and just have an R & R. We can stop anywhere we want to along the coast. We are both getting tired of this bad weather and not being able to travel more often. We both like the traveling part and we do meet a lot of interesting people along the way. The weather has been too bad to even think about going outside on the ocean.

Fenwick Island Anchorage, South Carolina
December 3, 2013

We are in an anchorage right now waiting for the right time to navigate another problem area in the ICW. It seems there are many. Yesterday we went under our first bridge that had a 64 ft clearance and we didn't touch! So now we are in South Carolina, a short day's run from Beaufort. We plan to hang out there for a little while to rest up. This traveling every day is rough, but we've been having some beautiful days—finally! Every day we spot dolphins, sometimes quite close. We try to get photos, but they appear and disappear so quickly that it is almost impossible. We don't remember seeing so many 28 years ago until we got farther south, but then there is a lot we don't remember about passing through this area 28 years ago. (There's a lot we just don't remember about 28 years ago!) We will spend Christmas in Beaufort, we plan be there for a month and then head on south again. It will be good to stop and regroup.

Beaufort, South Carolina

Dec. 4, 2013

We made it through the Ashepoo-Coosaw Cut (don't you love the name?), the latest ICW trouble spot. We waited at Fenwick Island for high tide, and as we were waiting, a huge double barge with a tug at both ends came through. We figured that they had timed it for the high tide, too, and if they could make it we could. Well, our lowest depth reading was 9 feet. Take away 7 feet for the tide, and at low tide there would have been just two feet of water in the cut!

Today we finally got to shed our long underwear, watch caps, 2 pairs of gloves, 2 layers of clothes, winter jacket, heavy socks, and scarf. So much for balmy, tropical weather. This is an unusually cold fall on the East Coast. We traveled at the same time 28 years ago and according to our log the weather was great. While we are laying over Jim is baking bread. We have the luxury of having an oven. I made a blueberry crumble cake earlier. Jim made the most delicious omelet with potatoes, onions, white cheddar cheese, and roasted red peppers.

When we're in an anchorage or at a dock, we can bake and cook because we have the time. When we're moving, our time is spent reading charts, plotting courses, and being alert and aware of boats, tides, floating objects, and following the coastal markers so that we don't go aground. Navigating is a full-time job. Then when we're sailing, that's another story. I get to take photos when I get tired of being at the helm.

Chapter Eight:

Held Captive in Beaufort, SC

Angie: As soon as we tied up at the dock in Beaufort (that's Bew-fort in South Carolina) we started meeting other boaters and having great conversations. The locals are very friendly to boaters and go out of their way to make us feel at home. We hang out at a bar called "Luther's" and were quickly known by the bartender and wait staff. Originally a pharmacy founded in 1906, the bar's motto is "Good for what Ales you." It felt good to land someplace after several stressful weeks on the waterway, and we aren't sure when we will leave. We both felt that we made the right decision to stop here for a month and recoup from all that nasty, cold weather we had to endure. The sun felt so good.

Beaufort is a wonderful small town with lots of culture. We were in time for a big Gullah performance/celebration that takes place in Beaufort every December. The Gullah are descendants of slaves who inhabited the islands that make up the coast of South Carolina between Charleston and Savannah. Because the climate was so miserable and the regions infested with mosquitoes carrying malaria and yellow fever, the white slave owners lived apart on the mainland. As a result, the Africans developed a distinctive culture that is honored and carried on by their descendants.

Pat Conroy, the author of *Prince of Tides*, is from Beaufort and taught school on Daufuskee Island where many of the Gullah live. In his memoir "The Water is Wide" he tells about trying unsuccessfully to teach the kids to swim. Many of the Gullah had had bad experiences with power boats coming through from the North. Hence, the Gullah children were terrified of the "Snowbirds" and wouldn't go in the water.

We can't tell you how many people we met in Beaufort who told us, "We came here in (name a year) planning to stay (a few days, a week, a month) and here we still are, x years later." We can see their point. We arrived in Beaufort on December 3rd, and though we planned to leave and continue farther south, we signed up for another month, and then another, at the Downtown Marina. Beaufort is a captivating town, claiming to have been named "the happiest coastal town in the East."

Beaufort begins to charm you as soon as you land at the elegant waterfront park with its palm lined brick walkway along the Beaufort River, part of the Intracoastal Waterway. (This was all new since our first visit to Beaufort aboard *Escapade*. At that time we had to land along an oyster encrusted wooden pier and managed to put a hole in our inflatable dinghy.) From the waterfront park you stroll through "The Point," densely packed with pre-Civil War mansions built by the owners of the Sea Island plantations where their black slaves raised the indigo, rice, and cotton that at one time made Beaufort County the richest county in South Carolina. Walking among the mansions on streets punctuated with mammoth oaks draped with Spanish moss, you feel transported into another place and time. You can understand why so many movies, including *Forest Gump, The Big Chill*, and, of course, *Prince of Tides*, have been filmed here.

The history became even more real to us when we entered a gallery and antique store on Bay Street advertising art by four generations of a family who at one time were numbered among the local planters, as they called themselves. "Our family, like most of the planters here, treated their slaves very well," they told us after I had softened them up with some friendly chatting. "It was overseers who were responsible for the abuses you hear about." They apparently didn't see the irony. The owners of the island plantations didn't live on them, but instead built winter and summer homes where the climate was more bearable and diseases like yellow fever and malaria less prevalent, leaving the management of the slaves who worked the plantations to the overseers. As a result, the black people who worked the plantations developed their unique dialect and subculture known as Gullah. When the Union troops occupied this area, in the early days of the Civil War, the owners mostly abandoned their lands, and the Gullah became among the first slaves to be freed when they were taken as "contraband" by the Union general. Many of them fought for the Union in the war, and one in particular, Robert Smalls, became a local hero. Captain of a merchant ship working out of Charleston, he gathered together family and friends and under cover of darkness snuck the ship past the Confederate barricades and delivered it, and his fellow slaves, to the Union army in Beaufort. He went on to serve three terms as a U.S. Congressman. The Gullah are extremely proud of their heritage and add a distinct flavor to both the food and the culture of this region.

The historic part of Beaufort covers about a square mile, and one of the great attractions for us was that the marina where we were staying is right on the main street, within walking distance of some great restaurants, bars, and art galleries. And we did walk. So much that we were recognized and greeted by many of the locals. And that's another attraction. People we'd never seen before smiled and said "Hello, how ya doin'" when they passed us on the street. It's an uncommonly friendly town, and that's partly because "local" is a relative term here. It seems like eighty percent of the people we met have a story about how they ended up in Beaufort two or ten or twenty years ago. Of course there are natives here, but for the most part they seem to welcome rather than resent the newcomers. It's as though the indigenous small town Southern friendliness is a virus that infects all who come in contact with it. We happened to mention to Larry Davidson, a local resident who had a boat across the dock from us, that we had some errands to do but that the marina courtesy car wasn't available. "Take mine," he said. We had to ask his last name in case we were stopped and had to explain why we were driving a car belonging to someone else. Larry became a great friend and one of the reasons we stayed in Beaufort as long as we did. Joe Bonturi was another permanent resident who befriended us. Joe lived on his boat *Nirvana Blues* tied up right behind us at the dock. A licensed captain who has delivered an untold number of boats everywhere from Maine to the Caribbean and who also worked for NOAA in California for many years, he seems to know everything there is to know about boats. He had rebuilt *Nirvana* from the inside out. He helped us and anyone else at the marina whenever we had a problem with the boat and would accept no more that a six pack as compensation.

John Marshall, a professional chef who also lives on his sailboat here in the marina, is another one of the people who ended up landing in Beaufort. Born in Detroit, he has lived in Florida, San Francisco, New York, Germany, and Virginia and traveled to Morocco, Argentina, Spain, France and Italy. John opened a small restaurant/bar in town called the Old Bull. The Old Bull was "closed" on Mondays, but the bar was open to all the local wait people and musicians, who usually have Monday nights off. Everyone who came in got a cup of John's gourmet soup of the night along with their drinks. And in case you should ever visit Beaufort, the Old Bull has the most delicious food at the best prices in town.

Because Beaufort County is made up of low-lying islands, bordered by tidal marsh lands, it hasn't become over-developed. Yes, there is Hilton Head, and there is a scattering of gated communities, but much of the area is in its natural state. Hunting Island has been preserved as a state park. Driving its winding trails through the mixture of palms and moss draped live oaks, you feel like you are entering a primeval forest. It is a mystical, magical place. You half expect to see dinosaurs emerging from the trees by the lagoon.

Jim's journal: This morning I get up and look out at the harbor where the sun is just beginning to chase away the light mist lying over the flat water. I think that there is no place that I would rather be right now. So, yes, we will soon head out to experience some new territory. But not today.

It was March before we uncleated our dock lines and, waving goodbye to our friends at the dock, headed south again.

Chapter Nine:

Over the Bounding Main

Jim: We are sitting in the mooring field at Fernandina Beach, rocking and rolling in gale force winds. A few minutes ago our cabin heater, which kept us warm and toasty at 74 degrees last evening, blew out in a back draft and filled the cabin with smoke. For a moment I wasn't sure whether or not we would have to abandon ship, but within minutes all of the fuel sources were shut off, and the cabin was clearing with the help of a few open ports and fans going. We are safe, but the cabin temperature has dropped from 68 to 64 degrees. We will have to live with the warmth that our trawler lantern gives off, since we won't be able to use the cabin heater in these winds. I'm not sure that we'll be able to trust it at all anymore. But we ARE safe, and managing to stay reasonably warm with long underwear, blankets and hot water bottles. But who'd have thought that we would be getting this kind of weather in Florida?

We had cheered when the weather forecast gave us a window to make the passage from Beaufort to Florida on March 1 and 2. We were ready to leave Beaufort for new scenery and very excited about making our first ocean passage on *Bel Canto*. We figured the passage from Beaufort to Fernandina Beach would take us somewhere between

22 and 26 hours, and no strong winds or threatening weather patterns were predicted for the next two days.

Saturday, March 1, dawned clear and relatively warm. We were up early, disconnecting power cords and making sure everything was stowed securely for our trip. We needed to leave the dock before nine o'clock to take advantage of the rising tide and incoming current for an easy departure. Joe Bonturi, our neighbor on *Nirvana Blues*, was there to give us a hand off. We pushed the bow away from the dock and glided off into the perfect morning. There was just enough breeze on the river to have us looking forward to raising the sails as soon as we cleared the McTeer Bridge, just a couple of miles downriver.

What we hadn't counted on was the tide, always higher after a new moon, being two feet above normal. As we approached the bridge we could see that the water was high on the bridge stanchions. Angie got the binoculars and looked for the gauge that would tell us the bridge clearance. There wasn't one. We slowed the boat to a crawl while I checked all of our references for information on the bridge clearance. They all gave the clearance at 65 feet without any mention of problems. Angie gave me a questioning look, and I said, "We'll go through." I started to crawl forward at idle speed, all the time looking at the stanchions with their bases awash. (It doesn't do any good to look up—the mast always looks like it is going to hit!) At the last moment I was seized with doubt and wheeled the boat around.

The Port Royal Landing marina is located just before the bridge. I radioed to see if I could get any more information on the bridge clearance. "We've been watching you," they radioed back. "We're looking at the bridge fenderboards with binoculars and right now the clearance is 63 feet." They told us how to gauge the clearance by the number of boards showing on the channel fenders. There was nothing for us to do but thank our lucky stars or the sea gods that I hadn't been foolish. We headed back to Beaufort to wait for the tide to go out. Back in Beaufort we tied up at the fuel dock and took advantage of the delay to breakfast heartily on a Spanish omelet and bacon. Good thing. This was the last real meal we were to have until we arrived in Fernandina Beach.

Jim at the helm

Shortly after noon we headed out again, and soon we had cleared the bridge with feet to spare. The sky was clear, the breeze fair. We put out sail with joy in our hearts as we pushed out into Port Royal Sound, scurrying along on the outgoing tide. Several dolphins surfaced near the boat as if to confirm our good luck. As we headed down the sound toward the ocean, though, the wind began to weaken. Going out the long channel that leads out of the sound past the shoals on each side, we were again under power. It was nearing four o'clock when we had cleared all of the breakers that lay just outside the channel and turned on the course we would be following for the next 80 miles. For the next few hours we "motorsailed" (sails up but motor running and giving us most of our momentum), the sails helping to steady us against the three to five foot waves hitting us abeam. The wind gradually died out, though, and the boat's motion became more and more uncomfortable. Sailboats are designed to sail (obviously), and the combination of sail and keel give them more stability in a seaway than a comparable power vessel would have. But when just under power, the height and weight of the mast and rigging accentuate the rolling, and this was the case on *Bel Canto* for most of the night. Since we both felt more comfortable above deck than below, and since we were only going to be out for one night, we decided to forgo watches and keep each other company in the cockpit. Ten CD's by our favorite singers playing over the cockpit speakers would help to keep us in the awake mode.

Fortunately the night was clear, though fairly cold. As we looked at the star filled sky, undimmed by any loom from light sources on shore, we recalled that one perfect night of ocean sailing many years before when our friends John and Zelda had joined us for the passage on *Escapade* from Marion, Massachusetts, to Cutler, Maine. With the wind at about 12 knots astern we had sailed under spinnaker for thirteen hours, gazing at the August meteor showers among the stars overhead and at the two V's of diamond studded phosphorescence trailing off our stern. It was memories like this that had drawn us back to the ocean. As this night wore on, dew began to collect on the decks and the cold began to creep into our bones. Soon we were wrapped in blankets and clutching hot water bottles to keep warm, bracing ourselves against the motion of the boat and waiting for the long night to end.

By sunup the seas had quieted a great deal and we were feeling much more upbeat. But as we approached our goal, the weather had one more little surprise for us. A thick fog blanket descended along the shore, reducing visibility to a few hundred feet. NOAA weather radio predicted that it would burn off by nine o'clock, so for a while we motored back and forth, being careful to keep out of the shipping lanes. By nine, though, there was no sign of the fog abating. We remembered that night when we arrived at Cutler under similar circumstances many years before. Then, Angie had guided us in, standing on the foredeck and directing me by listening to the bell buoy that marked the middle of the channel. Now, though, we had GPS and a modern chart plotter to help us. We determined that we could keep just outside the channel on the south side, keeping clear of both shoals and shipping lanes, and make it into the ICW safely.

A short time later we were safely (and quietly) moored at Fernandina Beach. We were dead tired, but feeling good about our achievement. Not that we had conquered a bit of the ocean. You don't conquer the ocean. Not that we had survived the trip, because we were never in survival mode. But we had raised the bar a little bit higher and accomplished our goal by making a short ocean passage. And that was a great feeling.

St. Augustine
Sunday, April 20, 2014

Our next stop was St. Augustine and we ended up staying more than a month. This was an experience much like the one we had in Beaufort, South Carolina. That is, we quickly became a part of the sailing community at the docks, and we had mixed feelings when it came time to say goodbye. Angie is still part of the St. Augustine sailors Facebook group and keeps track of the comings and goings of the friends we made there.

Right on the intracoastal waterway, St. Augustine has become a magnet for cruisers and has an active community of sailors, some who come and stay for a few days a year, some for months, and some for years. One of our cruising friends said you can leave but it's like a bungee cord, pulling you back to it. It is home port to every kind of boat imaginable, including, when we were there, the Spanish galleon *San Pelayo*, replica of the ship sailed by Pedro Menendez de Aviles, St. Augustine's founder. The beautiful square rigger, which sailed here from Spain and has spent years cruising the East Coast before returning to its homeland, calls St. Augustine its home port in the Americas.

What makes St. Augustine so attractive? The oldest continuously occupied city in the United States (since 1565), under the flags of four nations, Spain, France, England, and the United States (and one wannabe, the Confederate States of America), it has to rank with New Orleans, San Francisco, Charleston, Savannah and Boston as one of the most interesting cities in the country. Truly impressive buildings, some authentically ancient (by American standards) like the Castillo de San Marcos, the fortress guarding the inlet from the sea. Some in the Spanish Renaissance style built as hotels by Henry Flagler, cofounder with Rockefeller of Standard Oil. And, as we said, a friendly community of sailors always ready to meet for happy hour.

Chapter Ten:

Heading North

Angie: For us, a month passed in St. Augustine before we knew it. We decided that this is as far south as we needed to go for this year, and planned to head back to the Chesapeake, and possibly on to Maine, for the summer. Our plan was to head north at a leisurely pace, taking time to explore and enjoy the anchorages that we had passed through or passed up on our way south. We aimed to follow the advice of our friends on the boat *Cinderella*—we didn't want to be any farther north than the azaleas were in bloom. What a luxury to look forward to longer days and warmer nights as we traveled, after the bone chilling cold we experienced on our way south in the fall. Our first day was a short one, about twelve miles or two hours to Pine Island. No hurry, so Jim had time to change the two fuel filters before we left. Always exciting, as we're never sure whether the engine will develop an air lock and refuse to run after we do this. But after a brief sputter the engine kicked in and ran smoothly, and by one o'clock we were heading through the Bridge of Lions.

It was a beautiful day, with dolphins swimming around our boat as we passed the St. Augustine inlet and headed up the waterway. By three o'clock we were anchored among the low lying islands and marsh grasses, sitting in the cockpit, sipping a beer, watching the herons and egrets and thinking what a great life this was.

Jim: The next day, Saturday, looked to be equally idyllic. The weather still beautiful, in the seventies, light breeze, sunny skies, a whole family of dolphins. The nearly full moon phase meant that low water came in the middle of the day, so none of the five bridges we had to pass under were going to be a problem. The only problem was that traveling on the waterway in Florida on a weekend is about like driving on I-75 or I-94. Sports fishermen and jet skiers buzzed passed us, often at close quarters, without regard to what their wake was doing to us, not to mention the water skier who kept falling right in our path. About three o'clock we reached our next anchorage, St. George Island, where we planned to spend a day exploring the plantation and poking around the marshes in our dinghy. What we didn't remember was that we had entered and left this anchorage on the way down at half tide, and what we hadn't counted on was the exceptionally low water caused by the nearly full moon. Angie has built in radar that tells her when to hand over the wheel to me, and this is what she did. As we headed into the harbor, *Bel Canto* came to a sudden stop. I can't say we were hard aground, because, fortunately for us, the bottom was soft mud, but we definitely weren't going any farther. We weren't too worried, because we were on a rising tide, and the light wind was blowing in the right direction to help us off when the time came. We motioned to a passing powerboat that had politely slowed as it passed us to come over, planning to ask them to speed by us creating a wake to help lift us off. But by the time they got near, the tide lifted us enough and the wind turned the boat enough that we were able to motor off. Co-captain Angie said there was no way that we were going to make it over the bar at the entrance to the harbor in the next couple of hours and that we should move on. There is no good anchorage near this one, but Fernandina Beach was only three or four hours away, so we decided to motor on. The water was still low, but after only one more close encounter with the mud, we made it through the tough spots. By evening we were moored at Fernandina Beach.

Angie's journal: After going aground twice on our way to Fernandina Beach, we decided to skip Georgia, which has even more "trouble spots," and do another 24 hour passage from Fernandina Beach, FL, to Beaufort, SC. Coming out of the Fernandina Beach Harbor making our way to the ocean was quite a ride because of the opposing tide and wind. We were crashing into the waves for at least an hour. If I had been on shore looking out at these waters, I would have said, "I'm not going out there!" Well, I was out there. *Bel Canto* is truly seaworthy, and she took the waves better than her crew. As we came out the long entrance channel, there was a clear line where the brackish river water met the ocean. As soon as we passed the line, the water smoothed out and we were able to sail comfortably.

This was quite a contrast to our earlier passage in the other direction. We were able to sail for several hours, breaking our previous record for time sailing. The winds were out of the East and sometimes on the nose, but the wave action was much better this time, and even when the wind was light, there was enough to fill our sails and help to steady the boat. I got two hours of sleep instead of a half hour and it wasn't as cold. At night we could see the full moon through the partly cloudy skies. We had a few lovely surprises, like the school of rays swimming just under the surface of the water, resembling nothing more than a squadron of fighter planes. Then I saw this orangish/ brown thing floating in the water. As we got closer, I saw that it was a sea turtle. It dived and then I saw this little turtle swimming just behind it. Sea turtles lay their eggs on the beach and then desert the eggs, so I don't think this was a mother and baby, but that's what it looked like. We saw another one swimming later on. And we had a whole pod of dolphins playing in the waves around our boat. We were pretty excited about seeing all these sea creatures.

By 0700 we were passing the entrance buoy in Port Royal Sound, and by shortly after ten we were anchored once more in Beaufort, South Carolina. All in all, it was a beautiful trip, the kind we live for.

Chapter Eleven:

Back up the Ditch

Friday, May 9, 2014

Jim: We had our plans all worked out for the next leg of our journey, from Beaufort, SC, up to Georgetown. This is a problematic stretch of the waterway, with several patches of low water and a couple of bridges we had to be careful going under. This meant getting just the right timing of high and low tides to have clearance on both ends. So we delayed our departure from Beaufort for a week to get it just right. (No problem—we love Beaufort!) Well, you know what Robert Burns said about the best laid plans of mice and men.

Monday, Cinco de Mayo, was a beautiful day to set out. We slipped our mooring just in time to make the nine o'clock opening of the Lady's Island bridge and passed under our first bridge with a good foot and half to spare over the tip of our mast. As usual, a few dolphins showed themselves as we were setting out, and in spite of a fair amount of traffic ranging from paddle boarders to jet skiers, we looked for a pleasant day on the water. The goal was to reach the notorious Ashepoo-Coosaw cut, a five mile stretch where we had calculated two feet of water at low tide, to pass through it on a rising tide and anchor for the night on the other side.

JIM & ANGIE GEORGE

All went well until we reached the Marine Air Force refueling station about an hour out of Beaufort. We were passing the Marine base dock when Angie noticed this guy in a life jacket frantically waving and yelling at us. We wheeled around to see what the nutcase wanted and were informed that we couldn't go through because the marines were conducting firing practice up ahead. No guard boat, no sign, just a guy on the dock waving his arms. He told us the firing would go on until noon, and that we would have to anchor some place and wait to go through. While we were doing that, several more boats came along and would have passed on through if we hadn't radioed them to tell them what was going on. One power boater was very skeptical of our "rumors" and kept spouting off on the radio about how this didn't make sense. Well, just before noon a marine launch did show up from the firing area and tell us that the firing would be over at one thirty. A little after one a power boat came through from the other direction, evidently missing whatever warnings the marines had placed on that end, and that ended their playing war. This put us three and a half hours behind schedule and would get us to the Ashepoo-Coosaw cut on a falling tide.

We started thinking of alternatives and decided that we could go down the Coosaw River and toward the ocean on St. Helena Sound, and then up the Ashepoo River. That would take us about an hour and a half more, but it was deep water all the way. We were a little nervous about it, since it was off the waterway and an unfamiliar route to us. As we passed the cut and headed down the sound, we radioed the crew on *Night Watch*, a smaller (and shallower draft) boat than *Bel Canto*, and asked them to tell us the depth of the bar when they entered the cut. *Night Watch* reported nothing less than seven feet, so we turned back toward the cut. I must have misjudged the entry, because as we went between the entrance marks, our depth gauge went to five feet and *Bel Canto* started slowing down. We must have plowed a furrow through the silt, because she kept going and soon we were back in 7 to 10 feet of water. The next day was a "normal" day on the waterway, and we set anchor in the Stono River, just South of Charleston, in order to take Elliott's Cut at slack tide in the morning. You might remember us writing about going through Elliott's cut on the way South. The current was four or five knots against us, and it took us 40 minutes to go a half mile. This time we breezed through on the end of the ebb tide, crossed Charleston Harbor, and in an hour or so we were back on the waterway. Our timing was perfect, rising tide for the problem areas, but not so high that we couldn't make it under the troublesome Isle of Palms bridge.

The day was hot, but it would have been a pleasant day, with dolphins surfacing next to the boat a couple of times. Would have been except for the plague of small black beetles that descended on us. They didn't bite, but they did drive us crazy landing on us and on everything around us. They usually died when we brushed them away, leaving an ugly yellow stain where they had been. At the end of the day, Angie must have cleaned up a thousand corpses. Fortunately a breeze came up and blew most of the beetles away. With a straight stretch of the waterway ahead, we were even able to sail for our usual 20 minutes. A little after three thirty we decided to stop for the night at the Awendaw Creek anchorage, about halfway between Charleston and our destination of Georgetown.

That probably wasn't the best decision we could have made. (I should say that I made.) Angie suggested that we could go on to the next anchorage, about fifteen miles up the ditch. It was high tide and there was a problematic stretch of water ahead of us. But that would have meant another two and a half hours on the waterway. I declined, thinking that the low tide the next day was at nine-thirty and that if we left by eleven we could still make Georgetown before the closing of the marina where we had a reservation. Miscalculation. Low tide was at eleven. We checked our log and found that on the way down we recorded six feet in this stretch at just past half tide (on a falling tide). So today we should be able to make it through a little after one. That meant we wouldn't make it to Georgetown, but what the hey. Georgetown would still be there tomorrow. That's what it's like, the good and the bad, on the waterway.

The Next Day

We had a five mile problem stretch of water ahead of us, sometimes called the McClellanville stretch, and to make it through we had to be on a rising tide. Shortly after noon, from our anchorage in Awendaw Creek, I could see a couple of trawlers heading up the waterway, so I radioed them to get a report on the water levels. The report was positive, and at a little after one, we hauled anchor and started up the waterway again. We tiptoed our way along for most of the five miles. I was steering and trying to judge from the inlets where the shoaling would be. Well, I misjudged (I should have followed the advice of my co-captain and just aimed for the next green marker). Suddenly the boat stopped, and the depth sounder showed three and a half feet of water under us. We were stuck. We were still on a rising tide, but a fairly stiff wind was blowing us toward shore, so I doubted if we would float off this time as we had before. We asked the crew of a passing power boat to go by us at full speed, hoping their wake would bounce us off, but they demurred, saying it wasn't their boat. After a few attempts to motor us off, I reluctantly called TowBoatUS in Georgetown for assistance. (We had insurance that covers this). We were told that their estimated arrival time was in 50 minutes, so in the meantime we set to work to do what we could to get ourselves off.

We've described kedging before. You load an anchor into your dinghy and drop it as far out from your boat toward deeper water as you can. Then you haul on the anchor and try to pull your bow around and work yourself off the bottom. This doesn't sound too difficult, but we had a stiff wind and a strong current to contend with. First we had to get the motor on the dinghy using the hoist on the stern of the boat. And remember, *Bel Canto* weighs sixteen tons! We were winching on the anchor rode with little success when another power boater came along and offered to create a wake for us. He did a great job spinning his boat on our shore side and creating about a two foot wake. After two passes we were able to pull ourselves off, just as TowBoatUS showed up. They helped us retrieve our anchor, which was stuck firmly in the hard bottom mud, and we were on our way again.

I was totally exhausted after that ordeal, and captain Angie took us to our next anchorage. On the way the dolphins rejoined us and seemed to be having great fun playing in our wake. Just before we reached the anchorage, Angie asked me to take the wheel. "Do you trust me?" I asked. "No," she replied, "but I have to go pee."

Angie's Journal: More Drama
Wrightsville Beach, North Carolina, Monday, May 19, 2014

There's never a shortage of drama. The day before yesterday we came into this spacious anchorage in Wrightsville Beach, NC. There were only a few boats and the weather was quiet. So we got up the next morning and there was a little blue boat, no name or registration number, anchored kind of close to us, but Jim thought it was going to be all right. Well, we get up this morning and when we look out, the boat is uncomfortably close. The wind is opposing the current, and when that happens, *Bel Canto* has the habit of riding up on her anchor chain. It is not all right—*Bel Canto* is about twenty feet from the blue boat. Jim starts the engine to avoid a collision, and the captain of the other boat comes up to see what is going on. Jim says, "We are too close. One of us has to move." Well, the law, or at least the custom, is that the first boat to anchor has the right of way, but this guy tells Jim that he is having a problem with his transmission. So we pull up the anchor and find a new spot. Anchoring in a crowded anchorage is not my favorite maneuver, but about an hour later we are set again in a spot far enough from all of the other boats. Then this afternoon, SeaTow brings in a disabled boat and they anchor about a hundred feet from us. Jim radioes the captain of the Sea Tow boat and tells him that he thinks they are too close. Sea Tow says that as long as we all swing the same way we'll be fine, but Jim tells him that that isn't what happens. SeaTow knows the rules, and reluctantly moves the disabled boat away from us.

After the excitement at McCellanville, we made it up to Georgetown without any problems. There's no good place to anchor there, and we had reserved a space at Hazzard Marine. Hazzard Marine has a face dock, a long pier parallel to the water, which I like because it makes it easy to dock the boat, and Susan, the dockmaster did a great job of helping us with the lines. Across the dock from us was the boat *Salt Shaker*, that had been on a mooring near us in Beaufort, SC. Walter and Gwen, the crew on *Salt Shaker*, told us about the drama in the mooring field in Beaufort that we had missed. The winds were blowing about 25 knots, and a boat anchored just outside the mooring field began to drag into the mooring field. It just missed *Salt Shaker* but dragged into a boat near them and did about two thousand dollars worth of damage. This boat also had a faulty transmission. TowBoatUS towed them to the town dock, which made the rest of the boats in the mooring field happy.

From Georgetown we went up the waterway and anchored in Bull Creek, one of our favorite anchorages on the Wacamaw River. It is a fairly deep creek, fourteen to eighteen feet all over, and surrounded by trees, so a lot more protected than the marsh grass anchorages farther south in South Carolina. We were all alone, but the next morning as we were pulling up anchor, *Grace*, another blue hulled double ender like *Bel Canto*, passed us. They had come in when we were below and anchored farther up the creek. We met them later in Southport and they told us that when they came into the creek and saw us they said, "Look, we are already here."

In Bull Creek we studied the waterway on up to Southport, NC. We decided we'd rather avoid all of the shallow spots and problem bridges, so we back tracked to Georgetown and anchored in Wynyah Bay, near the ocean, waiting for the right time to make another ocean passage so that we would arrive in Southport after daylight. At five thirty we pulled up the anchor. It took us two and a half hours against a two to three knot current to make it out into the ocean clear of all of the shoals, but we made it before dark. We had a southwest wind of about 10 knots and were able to sail for about four hours and motorsail the rest of the way. It was a pleasant sail under a full moon. We got into the channel of the Cape Fear River around seven a.m.

The manmade harbor at Southport is tight with fairly shallow water. We had hoped to dock at the face dock, but the harbor master told us he was saving that for "bigger boats," and directed us to a T-dock behind a big catamaran. It was a tight turn, and Jim was going as slowly as possible, as he always does. The wind caught the bow and we could see we weren't going to make it. Jim threw the boat into reverse. *Bel Canto* has a mind of her own in reverse, and as we neared the bank behind us we hoped that there was enough water that we wouldn't go aground. Jim got the boat turning the right way, I threw the dock hand a spring line, and we eased in behind the catamaran.

Southport turned out to be a timely stop. When we plugged into shore power, we discovered that our inverter/battery charger had crapped out. We already knew that the pump to the hose that we use to clean the mud off the anchor chain had failed, so we got them both replaced. Steve, the service manager, and Jeff, the electrician, knocked themselves out and we were soon ready to go again. Jim thought he had died and gone to heaven because he no longer had to dip a bucket to wash down the anchor chain.

At first I didn't care much for Southport. After we arrived we set out looking for a breakfast/lunch place. We walked about a mile before we found a place called "Locals," the only place that serves a full breakfast in Southport. By the time we got there we decided that lunch was more appropriate and ordered fish and chips. Most of the food on the menu was deep fried, not our usual fare, but hungry and dead tired after a night on the water, we just needed food. So my first impressions of the town weren't very good. But on the way back to the boat we passed a place called the Wine Rack. We stopped in and the owner told us about the Friday night wine tasting. He showed me the list of featured wines, a pinot noir, pinot grigio, chardonnay, Barbera, and a Tempranillo, all my favorite wines. I told him we would be back. He also sold premium coffee, and we bought a pound of my favorite Guatemalan. Then we kept walking and discovered the really cool section of Southport, down by the river. After we rested up this was where we hung out. We had some great sword fish, salmon, and grouper dinners at the Fishy Fishy and at Provision Seafood. They are both funky little places that reminded me of Key West in the Seventies. We listened to some great music at Fishy Fishy by two guitarists, one of whom had been on the road with Tina Turner among others.

The Friday night wine tasting was another hit. It cost five dollars a person, but if you bought a bottle of wine you got the five dollars back. They had great snacking food, crackers and cheese, salami, chips, spinach dip, and salsa. A glass of wine was five dollars for a generous serving. We ended up getting a bottle of the Barbera. So after further exploration of the town, I changed my opinion. Good food, good wine, good music and kind people will do it every time.

A Sigh of Relief
Beaufort, NC, May 24, 2014

When we reached Beaufort, NC, (bow-fort, as opposed to bew-fert where we spent so much time during the winter), we felt like we were done with the worst part of the ICW although we still felt some trepidation because you never know what the waterway has in store for you. We had spent two nights in the village of Swansboro, gathering our courage for the transit through Bogue Sound. Many "thin spots" in the water and one serious grounding just before reaching Mile Hammock Bay on the Camp LeJeune Marine Corps base, our intermediate stop between Southport and Swansboro, had rattled the skipper's nerves, so we took a day off to do some boat maintenance and explore the village.

Bogue Sound is a wide body of very shallow water with a very narrow channel through it and a couple of shoaling areas. A cross wind had the skipper a little nervous about the 20 mile transit, but we made it through without incident, with Captain Braveheart doing much of the steering. So when we were anchored in Town Creek Marina, we looked forward to a good dinner at the Aqua restaurant and a quiet night on the hook.

From Beaufort it was pretty much routine up the waterway to Norfolk, stopping at some of our favorite anchorages along the way.

One of these was Campbell Creek where we had spent three days in the fog on the way down, giving me the opportunity to get some great photographs, and another was Minim Creek, where Jim had made his favorite, "Sunrise on Minim Creek."

Chapter Twelve:

Hurrah for the Chesapeake

Saturday, June 7, 2014

Deltaville, Virginia, the Wicomoco River, Mill Creek at Solomons, Maryland. All quiet scenic anchorages, and the best part about it is that they are all in Chesapeake Bay. We are trying to do as much sailing as we can, but the wind doesn't always cooperate. We chose to motor into a stiff north wind and choppy seas yesterday in order to spend a day in La Trappe Creek, one of the prettiest spots we've seen. We're getting a lot of practice putting up the sails and taking them down. We don't mind. We're just happy that we're in deep water a lot of the time and don't have to duck under bridges.

We laugh now when we see a bridge. Wonder how much clearance there is on that bridge. Do you think we can make it? Get the binocs and read the gauge. There isn't any gauge. Look at the nav markers. Are we on a rising tide or a falling tide? What is the current doing? Is it flood tide or ebb tide? Was there a full moon? Hug the red marker in this spot. Don't come too close to the green marker. Take the outside of the curve. Yikes! This was our normal conversation on the waterway every day for several months. This doesn't include all the studying we had to do before we even started navigating each day. Then we would see dolphins and we knew that everything was going to be all right.

Bel Canto at anchor in the Chesapeake

La Trappe Creek—Island Paradise!

From Solomons, it was an easy day's run up to La Trappe Creek on the Choptank River.

From our blog: Today we got our first sighting of stingrays swimming in formation. With their fin tips out of the water they looked like schools of miniature sharks. So here we are in the paradise we imagined that we would find in the Bahamas or in the Caribbean. It is 80 degrees and the water warm so when we are done with the blog we will go for a swim. That will be the first. When we arrived last evening, we were the only boat here, though a couple of boats joined us later, so quietly that we didn't know they were there. And two families in runabouts came in today to enjoy the little beach. But what did we expect? It is a weekend, after all. We plan to spend two or three more weeks hanging out on the Eastern Shore and touching base in Annapolis. Then we will put *Bel Canto* on a mooring and go back to Ann Arbor for the summer.

From La Trappe Creek we headed on to Oxford to get some boat maintenance done before heading across the Bay to Galesville, where we had reserved a mooring. That included getting our fuel "polished," a process we felt was necessary because we had been going through fuel filters every fifty or sixty hours. To polish the fuel, they pumped it from our tanks into two fifty-gallon drums, then ran it through filters back into our tanks. This supposedly removed any debris and water that had made it into the tanks. We also foolishly believed that they would clean the tanks while they were empty. We spent a couple more more weeks hanging out on the Eastern Shore and then put *Bel Canto* on the mooring in Galesville. We planned to spend the summer months, when it is too hot and still for good sailing in the Chesapeake, catching up with friends and family and reacquainting ourselves with our house, and then come back to the Chesapeake and *Bel Canto* in the fall. (Of course, that summer turned out to be the exception and the weather in the Chesapeake was ideal.)

Back in Ann Arbor we relearned why we like the town so much. We heard lots of great music at the Kerrytown Concert House and the Zal Gaz Grotto, topped off with the Detroit Jazz Festival over Labor

Day weekend. Angie got to play Upwards with her friend Ruth, Jim got in some chess with his friend Dan and with the "old folks" at the Turner Senior Center, and we got to spend time with all our Michigan friends and family. After our renters moved out we took advantage of having removed all of our personal stuff from the living area to get a start on having some of our wood floors refinished and interior walls and cupboards painted. The ideal life for us, we decided, would be to become part time sailors, enjoying our Ann Arbor home during the beautiful Michigan spring and summer, and taking *Bel Canto* to warmer climes in the colder months.

Chapter 13:

Finale

We returned to *Bel Canto* in September (on the hottest day of the year) for what we expected to be another two months of sailing before we put *Bel Canto* to bed for the winter. The boat was in good shape after being on the mooring for two months, except that the bottom had become pretty foul from the growth in the brackish water of the upper Chesapeake. We also discovered that some water had leaked in around the compression post—another problem that we would have to solve. We made an appointment to have the boat hauled for bottom cleaning, and in the meantime we began to think about what she needed and what we wanted from her. We knew that we didn't want to take her down the waterway again and that short handed ocean sailing wasn't our cup of tea either. We loved the anchorages and the little seaside towns we had visited and enjoyed the friends that we made along the way. But *Bel Canto* was made for ocean voyaging, and we knew that wasn't for us. A smaller boat with a shallower draft and a shorter mast would have been a better choice. *Bel Canto* needed a few more things if we were to sail her up to Maine—radar, a life raft, a new whisker/spinnaker pole, and perhaps a new main sail. These would cost a fraction of what we had put into her, but it would still amount to quite a few boat units. Winter storage and maintenance could easily amount to four or five thousand dollars. We both came to the conclusion that it was time to sell *Bel Canto*. We contacted a broker in Annapolis who was delighted when he saw her. He thought that even though the average time a sailboat was on the market before selling was 304 days, we had a good chance of selling her during the October Annapolis boat show. We gave him a slide show that we had put together showing the boat along with a list of its features, including all of the improvements we had made in her.

In the meantime, we decided to sail back down to Virginia to avoid overstaying our welcome in Maryland (that is, the three month limit Maryland places on non-resident boaters). We had a great sail, one of the best of the year, sailing from Oxford down to Solomons Island. *Bel Canto* loves a beam reach, and at times we were hitting over eight knots (with a little help from the current). From there it was a couple of short hops down to Fishing Bay and Deltaville, Virginia. We didn't know that this would be our last good sail on *Bel Canto*.

Coming into Fishing Bay the engine started to flag and surge and we knew we were in trouble. After only thirty hours our fuel filters were clogging up. Since we were so close to port, Jim decided to put in a call to TowBoatUS rather than try to change the filters and bleed the air out of the fuel lines at sea. TowBoatUS didn't answer our call, but a good Samaritan on a nearby sailboat did. Skip Wylie, out for a sail with his family, came up alongside and said "I'm a mechanic. Can I help?" Skip tied up alongside and together we changed the primary fuel filter and bled the fuel lines.

We made it into the harbor without incident, the engine running smoothly once again. The next morning turned out to be a beautiful sailing day. The wind was steady out of the east, which meant that we would have a beam reach all the way up to Solomons. *Bel Canto* would be in her glory! But we were barely a half hour out of the harbor when the engine began to flag again. We made it back into the harbor and put in a call to Skip. Once again we changed filters and bled the injectors, all four of which were full of air. Since the filters were obviously clean, we decided that the culprit was an air leak caused by a piece of grit on the filter gasket that Jim had missed when cleaning the filter cup.

While testing the engine, Jim discovered something sparking in the engine compartment. He found that a wire pinned against the engine block by a hose had worn through and was creating a fire hazard. We didn't have the equipment (spare wire, connectors—we should have had them) to make the repair, so Skip came to the rescue again. In the process we discovered that even with all of the battery switches off, the wires were "hot." Skip thought that the problem might be a fault in the new inverter we had had installed in Southport. Since Zimmerman's Marine, the outfit that had installed the inverter, has an office in Deltaville, we thought we would get it checked out. To do so, we had to take the boat around Stingray Point into Broad Creek in the mouth of the Potomac River.

The weather turned against us. We sat at the dock in Broad Creek for two days, pounded by the north wind that barreled right into the harbor. The waves continually pounded *Bel Canto* against the dock making it the most uncomfortable two days that we had experienced. Finally the winds moderated enough, though still out of the north, that we thought we could make it up to Reedville, which would put us within striking distance of Solomons Island. Jim had used our last fuel filters in our battle with apparently contaminated fuel. None had been available in Deltaville, and we would have had to wait two more days for a special order to arrive, so we called ahead to West Marine in Solomons and bought all they had on hand on the spot, to be picked up when we arrived. We hated to travel without spare filters, but we crossed our fingers and hoped for the best. It was an uncomfortable motorboat ride to Reedville, bashing into two and three foot waves for four hours, but we finally made it into the very quiet and protected anchorage.

Our plan had been to make it up to the Seven Seas Cruising Club Gam being held in the Rhode River, just south of Annapolis, at the end of September. This annual event attracts cruisers from all over the world to attend seminars, share experiences and eat, drink and be merry together. But the wind stayed strong out of the north, with constant small craft and gale warnings, and we gave up all hope of making it in time. After four days, the winds calmed, but were still out of the north. We decided to make the best of it and motor up to Solomons. By late Sunday afternoon we were anchored in Back Creek. We raced to get the anchor set and the dinghy launched, trying to make it to the West Marine store before it closed. When we arrived, somewhat breathlessly, Angie opened the bag that the clerk had handed to Jim—and discovered that they had given us the wrong filters!

The next day was calm and we headed north again under power. Now we just wanted to make it back to Galesville in time to make a quick trip to Ann Arbor to help celebrate our friend Lou's 100th birthday. What's more our broker called to tell us that he already had an offer on the boat, and we had to get her back for a sea trial and survey. Incredibly, a couple that had already sold their home and were living out of their car while they looked for a boat had made an offer, sight unseen, based just on our slide show and description of the boat.

Angie: I was nervous about making the trip without spare fuel filters. Fortunately we have TowBoatUS insurance. They will tow you to a harbor if you have problems. We had never had to use that service, although they did help us get off a sand bar in the intracoastal. It was

42 nautical miles from Solomons to Galesville, about a seven or eight hour trip for us under power. We were moving merrily along, about halfway there when Jim went below, leaving me at the wheel. As he came back up into the cockpit, I heard a change in the engine rpm's. The engine slowed without me doing anything—not a good sign! We still had over 20 miles to go. I mentioned to Jim what I had heard, and he began listening too. The engine seemed to be running OK, then it began to slow again, and Jim shut the engine off. We were now adrift out in the middle of the Chesapeake, watching the big ships come by and hoping that they would see that we couldn't move out of their way.

We put in a call to TowBoatUS, and in about an hour Captain Rob came to our rescue with the towboat *Reliance*. After a five hour tow up the Chesapeake, he towed us right up to the dock at Bert Jabin's, with me at the wheel and Jim handling the lines, ready to jump onto the dock and brake the boat with a spring line. We didn't have to worry, it was a soft landing and soon we were secured to the dock at Jabin's Yacht Yard. We had picked Jabin's because we knew Ted could help solve our problems. We had come full circle. A year earlier Ted had worked on *Bel Canto* for four months getting her ready to sail, and now he would be helping us get her ready for her new owners.

Ted checked out the fuel tanks and we discovered that they had never been cleaned. He cleaned them and polished the fuel again. He also repacked the stuffing box, where the prop shaft goes through the hull. We had had that job done by the same people that supposedly cleaned our fuel, and that job hadn't been done properly either. With the help of Dave, our rigger, we learned about the drain hole at the base of the mast. With every heavy rain, water had been running down into the cabin from the compression post that supports the mast. I cleaned the drain hole and water poured out of the mast, solving that problem. When we left for Ann Arbor, the boat was ready for inspection.

Back in Ann Arbor, we waited nervously for the results of the survey and sea trial. We had to wait for the banks to reopen after Columbus day for the closing. We were on pins and needles, but all went well, and *Bel Canto* went to her new owners.

Afterword

Do we feel sad? Do we feel bad? Yes and no. It wasn't the adventure we had expected, nothing like our year aboard *Escapade* 29 years ago. We both got tired of the maintenance and expense of repairs. *Bel Canto* is a great boat, but she is over thirty years old, and that means she will always need something. And the stress of going up and down the waterway had taken its toll. We might have been happier with a different boat, one more fitted to what we were actually doing rather than what we thought we would be doing (that is poking around on the coast and hanging out in harbor towns, rather than ocean sailing). But on the other hand, we learned a lot, had some great times and made some great friends along the way. We will miss the boating life and when we visit harbors Angie thinks about going to sea again. Then she does a reality check and is happy with where she is.

We spent as much on making repairs and refurbishing *Bel Canto* as we had originally paid for her, replacing virtually every bit of original equipment that came with the boat. When we decided to sell her we listed all the changes we had made and put together a slide show showing her inside and out in great detail, and she was beautiful. Within a week we had an offer and after her inspection she went to her new owners, who planned to live aboard her indefinitely. In a way, we envied them. Angie's brother wryly remarked that we should have bought a boat from someone like us.

Bel Canto's selling price was more that we had paid for her, but far less than we had invested. A third of our time aboard had been spent at the dock doing repairs and additions. What we learned from the experience (aside from the fact that when buying a used boat you should have a high level of skepticism and take all of the surveyor's comments very seriously) was that you can't reproduce an experience that means as much to you as our year spent on *Escapade* had meant to us. But we had no regrets about our year on *Bel Canto*. We took some pride in returning *Bel Canto* to superb condition, in spite of the expense. We had interesting experiences, saw new places, and what was most important, made many new friends along the way. That, for us, was the best part of the cruising life. And although much of this book is a chronicle of problems we faced, as we put it together we were reminded of the quiet anchorages, sailing under the stars and moon, and all the beautiful sea life and wildlife we saw. That made it all worthwhile. We still dream about living aboard a boat somewhere, but realize that at our ages, and in the midst of a worldwide pandemic, the dream is better than the reality.

Glossary of Nautical Terms

Anchor

A note on anchoring.

Although the weight of an anchor is important, a boat is held in place not primarily by its weight. It is held by the anchor digging into or catching onto the bottom. For the anchor to work properly, the boat must be at an acute angle from the anchor. If the anchor is secured to the boat by all chain, as was the case with *Bel Canto*, the length of chain out must be three to five times the depth at the highest water expected, measured from the bow of the boat. If secured by a nylon rope (called a rode), as it was on *Escapade*, the length must be five to seven times the depth.

Some types of anchors mentioned in the text and how they differ.

> The **Danforth Anchor** consists of two pointed flukes that are hinged to open to about 30 degrees from the anchor shaft. The flukes dig into the ground when pulled from an angle. The Danforth is particularly effective when anchoring in sand. One drawback is that if the force on it shifts 180 degrees because of a change of wind or tide the anchor can pull loose, and it does not work very well on a weedy bottom.

A CQR or **plow anchor** looks like an old fashioned horse drawn plow blade with a fixed shaft. It is more secure (hence the name) than a Danforth in many situations because if the wind or tidal current changes, it tends to dig in again. Its main drawback is that in a soft mud or silt bottom it can plow a furrow through the bottom just as its name suggests.

The **Bruce Anchor** (also called a **spade** anchor) is based on a design used to anchor oil rigs in the North Sea and is very secure in most situations. It looks like a wide, slightly curved spade with the handle bent up at a 90 degree angle and then 90 degrees again. Once dug in, it is very hard to move when pulling at an angle. This anchor, which Angie bought for herself as a wedding present while on *Escapade*, served us well in the Bahamas.

The **Manson Supreme Anchor** is rated by Lloyds of London as a super safe anchor. It looks a little like a streamlined plow with a roll bar attached so that if it does pull out it will roll over and dig in again. This is the anchor that we relied upon on *Bel Canto*.

Anchor Rode The rope or line attaching the anchor to the boat

Beating A sailboat can sail at approximately 45 degrees into the direction the wind is coming from. Just as the air passing over the wings of an airplane lift it into the sky, the boat is pulled forward by wind passing over the sails. In a stiff wind this point of sail can be uncomfortable because the boat is bashing directly into the waves. (Sailors say its is the crew that is taking a beating.) This is also called sailing **close hauled**, since the sails are trimmed as close to the center line of the boat as possible.

Bear off, Bearing off Easing the sails out to move farther off the direction the wind is coming from. The opposite is **heading up**.

Berth A place to sleep, usually just wide enough for one or two bodies

Bight A loop in a line caused by it doubling back on itself. Also a section of a bay that resembles this shape.

Bilge The area under the sole (floor) of the boat. The lowest part of the bilge collects any water that gets into the boat.

Boat hook A pole with a hook on the end used for picking anything out of the water but mainly for snaring the line attached to a **mooring buoy**.

BOAT unit Acronym for Break Out Another Thousand. Boaters joked that it didn't hurt so much when you thought about the money you were pouring into maintaining your boat.

Boom A spar extending horizontally from a mast to hold the bottom edge of a sail

Bosun's Chair A sling used to hoist a person up a mast

Bowline A type of knot used to make a secure but easily untied loop in a line

Broad Reach Sailing with the wind coming over the stern quarter and the sails eased. Generally smooth sailing.

Bulkhead The wall or barrier between one section of the boat and another

Charts. Maps used in navigation showing depths and obstacles in the water

Chart Plotter. GPS with a screen at the helm showing a facsimile of the chart for the area. It is possible to designate a route with the chart plotter for the boat's steering system to follow. It will also keep track of and save the route sailed.

Chop Short, steep waves very uncomfortable to sail in

Clove hitch An easy to undo knot used to secure a line to a piling

Cockpit The area in the stern or sometimes in the center of the boat, lower than the deck, from which the boat is steered and lines handled.

Cockpit locker A locker under the seat on each side of the cockpit. On *Escapade* there were quarterberths next to each of the cockpit lockers.

Companionway Main entry from the deck to the boat's interior. A narrow hatch with a ladder extending down into the cabin. Our rule was that any guest(s) aboard the boat had to fit through the companionway hatch.

Compression Post A post between the deck and the keel to bear the downward force of a mast stepped on the deck

Draft The depth of water needed for the underwater part of the boat

Drew See Draft. To say the boat drew five feet was to say that it needs a depth of five feet.

Fairway A lane in a mooring field or anchorage kept open for the passage of boats. Not a good place to take a shower in the nude.

Fender A cylindrical shaped, air-filled cushion used to keep a boat's hull from bumping into a dock or another boat

Fin keel A keel that does not go the length of the hull but extends downward (like a fin) from the bottom of the boat. There is a space between the fin keel and the rudder, which may be attached to a **skeg**.

Furl The mainsail is furled along the boom when not in use. The foresail (genoa or jenny) may be furled on a roller attached to the forestay. This was the case on both *Escapade* and *Bel Canto*.

Galley The cooking area

Genoa The sail in front of the mast and attached to the forestay. Also **Jenny**

Gunnel A wooden or metal railing along the edge where the deck meets the hull

Halyard A line used for raising a sail up a mast

Hawsers Large lines used on barges, tugboats and ships

Heading up Pointing the boat more into the wind. The opposite is **bearing off.**

Heeling The boat leaning to port or starboard because of the force of the wind on the sails. Sailboats heel when heading into the wind.

Helm The position from which the boat is steered. *Escapade* had a **tiller** at the helm. *Bel Canto* had a wheel.

Hove to The sailboat put into a relatively stationary mode by reversing the foresail and easing the mainsail. (Sometimes by mistake if the crew isn't paying attention.)

Iron Jenny A slang term for using the motor on a sailboat when there isn't enough wind

Jenny Genoa. The sail in front of the mainsail and attached to the forestay.

Jib or Jibsail Another term for Genoa or Jenny

Kedge To use an anchor to free a boat that is aground. The anchor is set at a distance from the boat and the crew attempts to move the boat by hauling on the anchor. Also a type of anchor used on rocky ground.

Ketch A two masted sailboat with the shorter mast behind the main mast but ahead of the helm. A similar boat but with a smaller mast behind the helm is a **yawl**.

Knots Nautical miles per hour. A nautical mile (based on one minute or 1/60th of a degree of latitude) is just over 6000 feet.

Lee, leeward The direction away from the wind. The opposite is **windward**.

Lines Ropes

Life lines A cable attached to stanchions surrounding the deck of a boat. Also a line from the cockpit to the bow of a boat to which a sailor might attach a safety harness in rough weather.

LORAN A navigation system developed by the Navy to determine a ship's position by triangulating radio waves

Man overboard pole A long fiberglass pole with a buoy and a flag attached. It is thrown to a person who has fallen overboard.

Mast A spar (pole) extending upward from the boat, to which a sail is attached

Mast step The place that the foot of the mast rests, either on the deck or on the keel of the boat. If it rests on the deck there is a compression post between the deck and the keel to bear the downward thrust of the mast.

Mizzen Sail The smaller sail on a ketch or yawl aft of the main sail

Moorings Any place to secure a boat, but specifically a chain connected to a heavy, permanently placed anchor with a buoy at one end to which a boat can tie up. (**moor**).

Plow Anchor An anchor shaped something like the old fashioned horse drawn plow

Quarterberth A **berth** (bunk) in the stern of the boat on either side of the **cockpit**

Rafting Tying up along side an anchored or moored boat where it is either too crowded or the depths are too great to anchor.

Reaching Sailing on any point of sail (relative to the wind) between **beating** and **running**. A **close reach** means sailing into the wind at greater than a 45 degree angle.

Reef(v.) To reduce the area of a sail exposed to a strong wind by lowering the sail and securing the bottom part (foot) to the **boom**. **Double reefing** is used to reduce the size even further.

Rode The rope by which a boat is anchored (There are no "ropes" aboard a sailboat—only sheets, halyards, topping lifts, etc. (Generically called **lines**)

Rolling hitch A type of knot used to secure a line to another line

Running Sailing directly downwind. In this case (and when on a **broad reach**) the wind is pushing the boat rather than pulling it forward. Normally slow going unless the winds are quite strong. In moderate or low winds a **spinnaker** can be flown to increase the speed. Alternately, the boat can be sailed **wing and wing** (with the foresail out in one direction and the mainsail out in the other).

Running Rigging All of the lines (**sheets** and **halyards**, topping lifts, etc.) used for controlling the sails

Seacock A valve in the hull of a boat below the waterline

Sheets The lines used for controlling or adjusting the sails

Shrouds The lines (usually stainless steel cables) used to hold a **mast** in place laterally (along with the **forestay** and **backstay** at the bow and the stern of the boat). Part of the **standing rigging**

Skeg A protuberance from the hull of a fin keeled boat to which the rudder is attached

Spade anchor See **Anchor.** The **Bruce Anchor** was the classic spade anchor.

Spinnaker The large colorful sail that you see flying off the bow of a boat sailing downwind. The Spinnaker is used mainly in light and moderate winds (except in a race, when things tend to get a bit crazy).

Spreader A brace used to hold a **shroud** out from the mast

Standing rigging The stainless steel cables used for holding a mast in place

Stays All of the lines holding the mast in place. The parts of the standing rigging

Stepping the mast Raising the mast and putting it in position on the **mast step**, then securing it with the **stays**

Tacking When sailing upwind (at a 45 degree angle to the wind) changing the boat's position from having the wind on one side to having it on the other. This is how a sailboat gets to a point directly upwind. (Angie sometimes called it zigzagging.)

Tiller A stick at the helm attached to the rudder used to steer the boat

Trawler A type of cruising power boat designed to move at a relatively slow but fuel efficient speed (usually 8 to 12 knots) based on the design of a fishing boat used to haul nets

Tripline A line attached to the head of an anchor to make it easier to retrieve from the bottom

Whisker pole A pole used to hold the **genoa** out when sailing **wing and wing**

Windward The direction the wind is coming from. The opposite is **leeward**.

Wing and Wing Sailing downwind with the genoa out on one side and the mainsail out on the other. A tricky point of sail because it is easy to backwind one of the sails by getting slightly off course. (Not something you want to do in a strong wind!)

Vee berth A bunk in the bow of the boat or forward cabin narrower at one end that at the other

Yawl A two masted sailboat with the smaller mast aft of the helm (Not to be confused with the way the people in South Carolina and Georgia address you)